CP lot 12⁵⁰

A DEATH IN ZAMORA

Only surviving photograph of Ramón J. Sender and Amparo together. Taken by a sidewalk photographer on a Madrid street, circa 1935. Courtesy of Concha Sender.

A DEATH IN ZAMORA

Ramón
Sender
Barayón

UNIVERSITY OF
NEW MEXICO PRESS
Albuquerque

"You have with you," a voice replied, "the melancholy of the crimes you did not commit and of the deaths you will not know how to face."

from *The Affable Hangman* by Ramón J. Sender

Permission acknowledgments and Library of Congress Cataloging-in-Publication Data may be found on page 196.

CONTENTS

ACKNOWLEDGMENTS

I WISH to thank the National Endowment for the Arts for making possible the completion of this book. Also I wish to give my heartfelt thanks to the following: Kim Chernin for her warm encouragement and advice; my American mother Julia Davis for a line-by-line edit of the first draft; Peter Carroll for his help on a final restructuring; above all, my wife Judith who returned with me to Spain and made contacts with my Spanish family easy and understandable.

I wish to acknowledge the collaboration of Fernando Primo Martínez in Zamora in conducting interviews and researching addresses of informants. Also, I would like to thank friends of my mother and Spanish relatives who gave unstintingly of their time, especially my aunt Concha Sender Garcés whose detailed recollections did so much to make this book possible, my cousins Magdalena and Melchora Maes Barayón for their unswerving loyalty to Amparo's memory and cousin Mercedes Kemp who corrected some of the translations. My first stepmother Elizabeth Sauzon, my aunt Marcelle, and my mother's sister Eugenia contributed vital details. Dionisia Diaz Cortes' children and her cousin María, my childhood friends Maruchi and Pepi Rivera, all added important information as well as Amparo's piano student María Uria. For details of prison conditions in Zamora I am indebted to Palmira Sanjuan, Leonor Martínez Robles and to Pilar Fidalgo Carasa as well as Dionisio Heredero. So many of my Spanish family assisted us that it is impossible to name them all here. All I can do is offer my sincere thanks for their collaboration and their warm inclusion of me once more in their lives.

I dedicate this book with love and admiration to my sister Andrea (Sister Benedicta, Order of St. Helena) who has carried Amparo's image faithfully all her life. Her return to Spain proved to me it was possible to reenter the land of our dreams, and her confrontation of our childhood nightmare set me an example in emotional and moral courage. This story is as much hers as mine. Without her love, her tender concern and prayers, I would not have been gifted with the invulnerability to disaster which I seem to enjoy.

Spain, July 1936

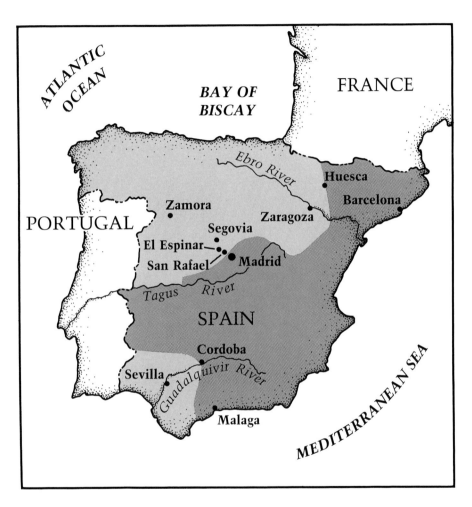

ATLANTIC OCEAN

BAY OF BISCAY

FRANCE

Ebro River

Huesca

Zamora

Zaragoza

Barcelona

PORTUGAL

Segovia

El Espinar

San Rafael

Madrid

Tagus River

SPAIN

Cordoba

Sevilla

Guadalquivir River

Malaga

MEDITERRANEAN SEA

Nationalist lines
Republican lines

AMPARO'S FAMILY

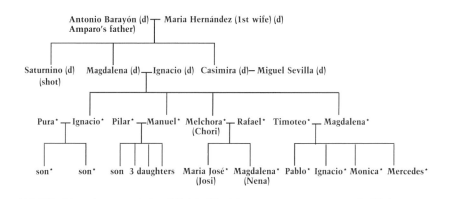

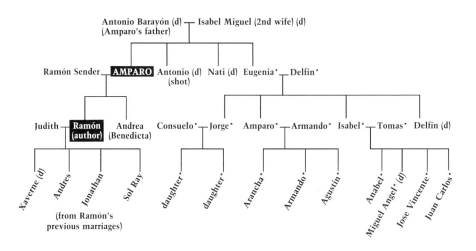

*Met by Ramón and Judith in Spain or France, 1983
(d) Deceased

RAMÓN'S FAMILY

MADRID FAMILY

- Conchita*
- Emiliano (d) (Emi)
  - Riqui (d)
  - Ana María*
    - Ana*
    - Fernando*
    - Jorge*
    - Ricardo*
    - Nacho*
    - Maca*
  - Fernando (d)

- Amparo (d)
- RAMÓN (d)
  - Ramón (author)
  - Andrea (Benedicta)

(see below for 2nd and 3rd marriages)

- Maruja (d)
- Guillermo (d)
  - María Aurora
  - Maribel

BARCELONA FAMILY

- Manolo (d–shot)
- Marcelle* (lives in Biarritz)

- Amparito (d)*
- Joaquín*
  - Joaquín*
  - Sheila*
    - Tamara*
    - Paula*
  - José Ramón*
  - wife
    - Ramón*
    - Joaquín*
  - daughter
  - María Elena*
  - (divorced husband)
    - Alva*
    - Hector*

José Sender
Andrea Garcés (d)

ZARAGOZA-JACA FAMILY

- Miguel Angel (d)
- wife
  - Carmen*
  - son*

- Angela*
- Rafael*
  - Rosa María
  - Rafael

- Eduardo (lost at sea) (d)

- Asunción (Suni)*
- Donald (d)*
  - José-Miguel*
  - Carlos
  - Daniela*

- Carmen*
- Pepe*
  - Inez*
  - Isabel (Babel)*

Ramón's second marriage:
Ramón (d) — Elizabeth*
Emmanuel — Irene
  Isabel   Thierry

Ramón's third marriage:
Ramón (d)—Florence

---

*Met by Ramón and Judith in Spain or France, 1983   (d) Deceased

xi

BEGINNING THE
SEARCH

WHEN my father Ramón J. Sender died, I thought all the horrible secrets of his life and my own would be buried forever. What really happened to his first wife, my mother? How had she died? Why had she been taken away? Who killed her? My father, the obvious person to ask, always refused to divulge any details. He was considered the greatest Spanish novelist of his generation, winner of the National Prize in literature in 1936, the Critics Prize in 1967, the Planeta Prize in 1969 and nominated for the Nobel Prize in literature in 1970.

My father died of a heart attack on January 15, 1982, just two weeks before his eighty-second birthday. Sorrow, relief, anger—awash in conflicting emotions I prepared to fly to his last home in San Diego. How could he die with so many unresolved questions hanging between us? And shouldn't I alert the Spanish family? I telephoned cousin Magdalena in Málaga with whom I had spoken for the first time only a month earlier. When her distant voice came on the line, I struggled to explain what had happened in my long-forgotten native tongue.

"*Papá es muerte,*" I said.

My fiancée Judy, in fluent Spanish, quickly corrected me. "*Papá se murió.*"

I had said, "Papá is death."

Yet in a sense I had spoken the truth. Throughout my life, my main contact with my father had been through his translated novels: *Pro Patria, Seven Red Sundays, Counterattack in Spain, Chronicle of Dawn, The Sphere, Dark Wedding,* and *The Affable Hangman.* They all contained a macabre element, a fascination with death that struck an alien tone within the "happily-ever-after" American culture which had absorbed me as a four-year-old refugee from the Spanish Civil War.

Throughout Franco's reign, my father refused to return to Spain. For thirty-five years most of his books went unpublished in his native land. In 1974, when the dictator lay more dead than alive in a final lingering illness, Papá allowed two visiting Spanish novelists to coax him home for a series of literary conferences. He was greeted in Barcelona by enthusiastic crowds. "SENDER RETURNS!" read the newspaper headlines. His life work, comprising more than eighty books, finally overcame the years of censorship and a new generation of Spaniards began to read them.

On his return to California that year, he told me that wherever he went, two bodyguards took the hotel rooms on either side of his. He had received death threats from both the far right and far left, and he warned me not to visit Spain under my own name. Yet I knew I had to go back. The thread through my particular labyrinth led across the Atlantic to Zamora, a provincial town in Old Castile. Must I risk my life to find it? To find my mother?

Time and again I begged my father for details about the death of my mother Amparo Barayón, but all my efforts proved fruitless. I even turned to hypnosis in the hopes of retrieving my earliest memories. One night a phrase in Spanish floated up from the depths: "*No quiero ir*"—"I don't want to go." I repeated it over and over. During the next hours I seemed to experience an event that had occurred forty years before, Amparo's arrest and my abandonment for what seemed a whole night.

The few definite facts I knew could be summarized simply: My mother Amparo had trained as a concert pianist, and my father had established a reputation as a novelist and radical journalist. They had met in Madrid, where I was born during "Red October" 1934.

According to my father, machine-gun fire from outside the clinic doors greeted my birth. Meanwhile, in the northern province of Asturias, General Franco's foreign legionnaires and Moroccan mercenaries were slaughtering the striking miners and their families.

One year later, my father had won the National Prize for literature for his novel *Mr. Witt among the Rebels.* The announcement had been made just before my sister Andrea was born and the February 1936 elections swept the Popular Front coalition into power. In July, army garrisons rebelled all over Spain. We were trapped in San Rafael, a resort that suddenly became the front lines. My father escaped on foot to the Republican zone and joined the militiamen defending the mountain pass. Over the next months he was promoted through the ranks to serve briefly as Chief of Staff for General Lister, a commander of the loyal Republican army. What happened to us and to Amparo lay buried under the changes of cultures, languages and families that followed.

A few weeks before Franco's victory in April 1939, my sister Andrea and I arrived in New York with our father. Andrea had just turned three; I was four and a half. Papá, penniless, placed us with an American war correspondent Jay Allen whom he had met in Spain. He departed at once for Mexico City to try to find a job and a home within the growing colony of Spanish exiles there. With the fall of the Spanish Republic, his passport was invalidated and he applied for Mexican citizenship. Because we were not Mexican residents, he could not include us on his application. As of that moment, we became children without a country, technically illegal aliens in the United States.

Meanwhile, Mildred Kenyon, a volunteer with Spanish Refugee Aid, searched for someone who would take us for a longer period, preferably someone with a house in the country where the fresh air and tranquillity would help us regain our health. She appealed to her friend Julia Davis, a woman who craved children without being able to bear them. Julia first agreed to take us for six weeks. The months became years, until it was tacitly understood she would bring us up as her own children.

Julia Davis, blue-eyed and slim with greying blonde hair, was thirty-nine years old at the time. Ever since her college days, she had devoted herself to writing. She gathered Nordic tales into a children's book and followed it with a novel for young adults on the Lewis and Clark expedition entitled *No Other White Men.* In the

1930s she worked as a journalist in New York and for the Children's Aid Society. Unable to place two of her older "cases," she adopted the children herself. Her novel, *The Sun Climbs Slow*, chronicled our informal adoption into her family. In it she presented a fictional version of Amparo's fate: a Spanish mother dies shielding her little boy from an exploding bomb. It was a gentle way, and the only way my father would permit, of telling us we would never see Amparo again.

Julia gave us all the love she would have given children of her own. By the time our father visited one year later, we could no longer understand Spanish.

"You have stolen my children," he said to her sorrowfully as she drove him from the airport to her home in rural Westchester County.

"*Je suis perdue*," Julia replied in French, their only common tongue, and proceeded to lose her way on a road she had traveled for years.

We remained with her even after Papá returned to the United States and married a woman named Florence Hall. They lived in New York for a few years, then settled in Albuquerque where he taught Spanish literature at the university for fifteen years. Occasionally we spent Easter vacations together, but our relationship remained distant.

What had happened to Amparo? All that remained of her was a full-face passport photo of a Spanish woman on the first page of our childhood album. It was a woman we did not recognize. She stared out at us with a sober expression, her brown, curly hair trimmed to her earlobes. I possessed only one other piece of evidence. As a teenager I found a yellowed, typewritten scrap of a press dispatch in Spanish in the box that contained our father's letters. It mentioned the death of Ramón J. Sender's wife and quoted her last letter:

> For myself, I do not care because I die for you. But the children. What will become of the children? In haste—
> Amparo

The summer I was fourteen the note disappeared. My father was visiting at the time, and my sister thought he destroyed it. However I remember carrying the fragment in my wallet as a boy, fondling it occasionally, sensing it contained a clue to the mystery of my mother's disappearance. Unfamiliar with Spanish at the time, I was un-

The photograph of Amparo which Andrea and I had as children. A passport or identity card photograph taken in 1936, with a dedication to Ramón Sr. on the back.

able to fathom it. Already fragile and torn, it may have finally decayed into shreds or I might have replaced it only to have Papá dispose of it.

As I grew older, I developed a curious obsession: whenever I visited a library, I invariably searched for one name: Amparo Barayón. I found a few references to "the wife of Ramón J. Sender" listed among examples of the ferocity of the fascist beast, but that was all. Constancia de la Mora referred to her in her book *In Place of Splendor*, a passionate account of a mother caught up in the Spanish people's struggle to save their Republic. It was one of the few books written by a woman about that era. According to someone who knew her, the author never forgave my father for abandoning us.

Despite my father's disapproval, I resolved to confront my only relative in North America, the one sister of my father who had emigrated to Mexico City. As small children, my sister and I had lived with her briefly in Barcelona. She showed me a photo of Amparo holding me as a newborn. My mother was dressed in a kimono with an orchid appliquéd to the shoulder. Here at last was the woman I remembered. The long slope of the cheek, the tenderness of her expression—in three-quarter profile she looked totally different from the person in the passport snapshot. The photograph became for me the first tangible evidence that Amparo had ever existed. I was almost forty years old.

My desire for her continued to grow. But to rediscover Amparo, I would have to battle my father's refusal to discuss her. On several occasions he specifically warned me not to write anything about her. I had no choice but to go back to the libraries.

At the University of California, I searched through yellowed newspapers whose pages crumbled under my fingertips. The Spanish headlines named battles whose outcomes had been decided long ago. The photographs showed crowds with their fists raised, their exuberant faces reflecting the optimism of the summer of 1936 when it seemed that the fascist generals would not conquer the nation. I raised my own fist, clenching the tendons tightly. A thrill went down my arm and my chest expanded. My body remembered that gesture! What word did I want to shout?

Perhaps I would find Amparo's face among the marchers carrying banners and chanting victory slogans. Somewhere a newspaper must have mentioned her. I fought the urge to search earlier issues and limited myself to late 1936 and 1937. Her name would not appear in the headlines but on some inside page. I was looking for some confirmation that Amparo ever lived. Even in the midst of Civil War Spain, her story could not have gone unnoticed.

Other images evoked a wordless emotion. On a poster, a muscular, bare-chested reaper bent over a sheaf of grain, blood pouring from a bullet wound in his thigh. In front of him, a grim, shirtless militiaman raised his shotgun to his cheek, ready to fire in defense of his brother. "COMRADES! WORK AND FIGHT FOR THE REVOLUTION!" the message read. I knew I had seen it before as a two-year-old walking through the rubble of a Barcelona street. I threw my fist in the air and whispered, *"Canalla!"* That was the word I wanted, the Spanish equivalent of "scum." I was addressing the Italian and German crews of the bombers which saturated Barcelona with death in March, 1937, eighteen raids in three-and-a-half days. According to my father, we had been there.

Another photo portrayed an empty-faced mother seated with her unsmiling children in a Madrid subway during an air raid. She might have been Amparo. In yet another photo, a line of women stood waiting for their milk ration. Their eyes stared into the sky to scan the insignia of the approaching planes, frowning against the light in an all-too-familiar grimace. Ours? Theirs? Thirty seconds later the street might disappear in an appalling thunderclap that would shear bones from their sockets and bury them under tons of debris. "Cousin Mary," "Aunt Pilar," "little Teresa" . . . each mutilated corpse threw a family into mourning.

After an unsuccessful search in Berkeley, I visited the Hoover Institute of War, Revolution and Peace at Stanford University, a good source of Spanish Civil War documents. In the basement archives, the librarian steered me to the collected papers of a certain Joaquín Maurín. His name seemed familiar. I opened a file box and understood why. It contained a foot-high stack of correspondence between him and my father spanning more than fifteen years.

Joaquín Maurín, founder of the Partido Obrero de Unificación Marxista (POUM), was taken prisoner early in the war by the fascists. Presumed dead by the Madrid press, a brigade was named after him. When he was found alive in a fascist prison, his wife worked ceaselessly to free him until at last he was released. They settled in New York where he started a literary agency and invited my father to submit articles for the Latin American press. His first letters were stiff and formal, as were Papá's replies. After they met, a warmth developed which blossomed into a close friendship. On one page he wrote:

> "I have met your children and am enchanted! Andrea is a charming lass, sparkling with grace and intelligence. And Ramón Jr. is a boy who speaks English but overflows with Spanishness in every direction."

Why don't I remember this extraordinary man? I have a vague recollection of "somebody Spanish" visiting us at Julia's. Perhaps my lack of interest concealed the depths of my pain.

In his letters, Papá occasionally mentioned me whenever I managed to elicit parental pride, such as when some music of mine was performed. Another letter told why he resigned himself to our remaining in Julia Davis's care, although the most important reason was "too romantic to tell." A long document locked in a Wall Street safe deposit box supposedly explained everything.

> "In it I also tell why the Russophiles—by Moscow's order—proposed to terminate certain people, among them myself. The others they killed after the War. So far they have not dared to try anything with me but it could be that they will try something. If something does happen to me, I don't want my children to suffer a new shock after having known so many in the Civil War . . . I will never forgive the Communists who have deprived me of one of the most legitimate satisfactions of life: to live with my children. . . . Obviously the children know nothing of this. The document must be withdrawn and published on the day anything happens to me. However I believe the Communists have renounced their original intentions and now follow what they call 'civil death,' that is to say, a systematic persecution by slander, etc."

If only he had told us his reasons for not living with us! Or sat down one day and gently described our mother's life and ultimate sacrifice. The truth of Amparo's disappearance, no matter how horrifying, would have allowed the natural mourning process to heal us. All we needed was some acknowledgment, some proof of her existence. But he saw us as living reminders of his greatest failure, his inability to protect his wife and children. He never understood our need to know the reality behind the evasions and lies.

Gradually I built a bibliography for my story. There was my father's book *Counterattack in Spain* which described his life during the last six months of 1936. Surprisingly, he did not mention Amparo's fate until, at the translator's urging, he included a few brief paragraphs on the final pages. According to what he once said, the heroine of his untranslated novel *The Five Books of Ariadne* was modeled after my mother. I began laboriously translating segments of Ariadne's life story. How much was truth, how much fiction? Over the telephone, my sister mentioned a woman character in another novel, *Seven Red Sundays*, supposedly based on Amparo. Also she gave me an address for Amparo's niece Magdalena in Málaga, someone she had met during her own brief return to Spain a few years earlier. I wrote to her the first time I had tried to contact someone in Spain myself.

How strange my letter must have seemed. The family only remembered a screaming, distraught two-year-old whose terror reflected their own. Yet if I could reach back through time and tell that child the true story of what happened, perhaps the cloud that obscured my memory of Amparo would dissipate. And perhaps the perpetual winter that existed between my father and me would thaw before death froze our estrangement permanently. I had to try, in spite of his insistence that I leave Amparo's story alone. After all, my affliction was also his.

In the final pages of *Counterattack in Spain* he writes: "I will silence, extinguish, the voices which rise clamorously and imperatively in my heart." Yet the very next sentence states: "I have always written with an indefinite need to reveal myself completely and impartially to the world and not to conceal myself." But were not Andrea and I part of the world? Was it a Spanish trait not to show emotion before your children?

A year before my father's death, I brought my fiancée Judy to San Diego for Christmas Eve dinner so that she could meet him and Florence. Since their divorce a dozen years earlier, they had evolved a unique routine: Papá lived as he pleased in his own apartment, while Florence hovered anxiously from her flat four blocks away, where he came for his meals. That evening, talk at the table had focused on the New York publishing scene.

"It's being ruined by the Jews!" he rumbled. "The last Jewish author of any consequence was King David of the Psalms."

I begged to differ, feeling that at the very least the remark showed no respect for Judy's Jewish background.

"Come on, Papá!" I coaxed. "I can think of at least a dozen Jewish authors worth a mention."

But the old man was in no mood to be contradicted. He stomped away from the meal and fired his parting salvo from the front door.

"Now I know, Ramón, that you have not yet grown up!"

When we returned home, I wrote him a conciliatory note saying that life was too short for misunderstandings. But his final remark, measuring my maturity by my agreement with his prejudices, remained in my thoughts. The reality of the situation was just the opposite: in order to "grow up," I would have to confront his refusal to give me information about Amparo.

I returned to the Hoover Library with renewed determination. On its shelves I found some of Franco's historians' texts. They gave their version of what they labeled "The Crusade." One book detailed hundreds of atrocities complete with photos of corpses in every conceivable state of dismemberment and decomposition. It was a hard book to look at. In America we are so protected from death that its emptiness confronts us like some alien creature. In Franco's death book, the faces reflected surprise, horror, ravished suffering, even an ethereal ecstasy as if in the last throes the pain had been transmuted into something indescribably blissful. But the dead children were the worst, open-mouthed with white tags around their necks.

I waited impatiently for my cousin Magdalena's answer, but nothing arrived. I decided to try telephoning. Why hadn't I ever called Spain before? During the Franco years I had become habituated to believing it was out of bounds. I listened with deep emotion to the operators speaking in Spanish. When was the last time I had heard Spanish women talk? There was so much drama in their inflections, so much humor as well. Amparo had worked for the telephone company. Perhaps her voice was like theirs, throaty and expressive. At last Spanish Information replied there was nothing. Either Magdalena's number was unlisted or she did not have a phone.

Meanwhile I pleaded with my father for material relating to Amparo. In response, I received a copy of Magdalena's first letter to him. But the letter did not come from him but from Florence who guarded his privacy as zealously as she could:

July 5, 1945

Dear Tío Ramón:

Only a few minutes ago I turned on the radio (Voice of America) . . . and you were speaking on the subject of American independence—such a blessed people! You have spoken the truth to the entire world—this tremendous truth of ours—which so many search for in vain. Many years ago I read an announcement of your death in the papers and my mother and I wept without ever having known you. But during a journey to Madrid in the winter of 1944, a countryman of yours gave me the stupendous news that you were living in Mexico City. I've searched for information about your whereabouts ever since. Finally today we learned unexpectedly that you are in New York. You cannot imagine the joy and emotions we experienced. . . . What worries us most of all is the fate of Monchín (little Ramón) and Andreita. Mamá often thinks about them and cries. It would bring us incredible joy to know that they are well. I was eleven years old when that happened. I remember Monchín was terrorized by the bombers, and cried in the hallway of the house at the slightest noise. My mother took him to a children's specialist. Both my parents suffered much at not being able to shelter them in our home. I lament that I cannot give you the reasons for this at this time. I will never forget the last time I saw Amparo. She was happy and talked about taking me to Madrid with her. She always was my favorite aunt and she loved me a great deal. When I showed her some things I had written, she said to me: "In a few days we'll go to Madrid. You'll come with me and your uncle will teach you how to become a good journalist, you'll see!" I remember everything she said so clearly. Since then, I have written more serious things which are at the point of costing me dearly. We have here the letters Amparo wrote. They are to me the best pages anyone has ever written. You cannot imagine how anxious we are to hear from you! Mamá doubts that you will reply. She says that it's possible you believe we are of the same sort as that man Sevilla. I have so many things to tell you! Since I was eleven when my eyes were opened so brutally I have done nothing but hate. For my family and for me especially your respect means a great deal. I have spoken several times with the woman who took Monchín to San Juan de Luz, trying to find out something, but . . . she knows nothing and remembers nothing. Do not delay in answering, please, and give me news of the children. Is it possible they are in Barcelona as Mrs. Maximina supposes? If so, give me their address and I will immediately go to see them. We have to do what is possible to give back the greater part of what they lost. He who committed the frightful deed has died. Wretchedly. Receive the love and the sincere admiration of all the family, especially from your niece.

Magdalena

The letter gave me more information than I might have hoped. What did "the same sort as that man Sevilla" mean? Who was "Mrs. Maximina?" The woman who took me to San Juan de Luz? And who "died wretchedly" for what frightful deed? Had my father received copies of Amparo's letters from Magdalena? There was some sort of cover-up going on. He might have been exiled from Spain for thirty-five years, but I had been exiled for a lifetime from even a single remembrance of my own mother!

A few weeks passed, my father still unwilling to communicate further. It was November 18, 1981: the forty-fifth anniversary of a date carved on the ornate family mausoleum in Zamora. In San Francisco where I lived, the sky sparkled a crystalline blue after the rainstorms of the weekend. This should be a day of darkness, I thought, of counting up blood debts still unpaid. I decided to try to find Magdalena again, this time by telephoning Zamora Information at two in the morning Pacific Standard Time.

Her letter had mentioned three brothers and sisters plus an oblique reference to an Antonio, so I asked the Zamora operator for Antonio Maes Barayón. Names repeat from generation to generation in Spain, so the odds were in my favor. She gave me a number! I dialed but the lines were busy. When I got through an hour later, the person who answered was the wife of Ignacio Maes Barayón, one of

Magdalena's brothers. I identified myself to this friendly voice and asked for Magdalena's married name and phone number. She gave me both and inquired after my father. I replied that he was well. Family stuff. How I hungered for these simple conversations that spoke the language of the blood!

Magdalena was out when I called, but a maid told me she would return from her shop at lunchtime. She had a shop! It was now four A.M. on my clock, one in the afternoon there. Maybe this was why Spain existed only in my dreams, because they were awake while I slept. When I phoned at six, Magdalena answered. At last I was speaking to my mother's niece! My poor grasp of Spanish did not allow me to express my feelings fully.

"I spent a week with your father in Madrid and told him everything," she said. "I gave him letters, documents and photos."

"Papá cannot talk about these things," I explained. "Do you have copies? Did you receive my letters?"

Magdalena's voice was not too friendly. "He does not want anyone writing about Amparo," she warned me. "But I'll send you everything I have."

Compared to Ignacio's wife, Magdalena definitely was cool. Had Papá warned her not to answer me? If there existed a Freedom of Information Act for families, I would have invoked it. In my fantasies I subpoenaed them both and cross-examined them under oath.

Curiously, in my father's novel *The Five Books of Ariadne*, Ariadne (Amparo) and Javier (Ramón) testify before a surrealistic tribunal. There he lists some possibilities of what could have happened to her:

> *The first possibility*
> Ariadne (Amparo), wife of Javier (Ramón), surrendered herself to the rebels.
>
> *The second possibility*
> One evening there came the horrible Herculana, and Quiñones, nick-named "Lizard." The house was full of papers which implicated her and they arrested her.
>
> *The third possibility*
> I, Javier, was guilty, through a type of deferred good faith, for having left those documents in reach of the authorities.

The fourth possibility
  She was also guilty, because she did not follow my instructions.

The last possibility
  Ariadne, in spite of everything, lives on, disgraced and amorous, in the style of her ancestors, but always young like the day we separated in Pinarel.

My search for Amparo continued. I drafted a fictional version of Amparo's story as best I could from what few sources I had available, mostly my father's novels and my imagination, and sent it to him with a carefully constructed letter of explanation. I hoped it would provoke a sympathetic response. Instead, my stepmother Florence replied, scolding me for disobeying his admonitions and disturbing him. A few days later, I received a letter from Magdalena. She would not help me. She said my father had everything—names, dates, documents, photos, but he absolutely did not want anyone to use them. She continued: "A short while after the dictator died, an important editor of this country gave me a blank check to write the story of your mother. I told him there wasn't enough money in the world to pay for a sad story of the accursed war about someone of my blood. I feel for you, but search in another place."

Nothing was left but to telephone the old man—the confrontation I had been avoiding ever since I began the book. I was positive Magdalena's refusal was all his doing.

"Magdalena will tell you nothing because there is nothing!" he shouted. "All you want to do is make money out of your mother's bones!"

I drew a deep breath. "If the book makes any money, I'll donate it to the Spanish Refugee Aid if that makes you feel better."

"Then you want attention! You are screaming for fame!"

I changed the subject to my upcoming marriage to Judy. I invited him to attend and, mentioned that Julia was planning to be there.

"Bah, you are crrrazy!" he growled. "Julia has no respect for you. She will never come."

"She says that she is," I replied, stupefied by his response.

His laughter rasped in my ear, edged with hysteria. "I tell you she will not! You are stupid, an imbecile! The truth is that she hates you!"

This had gone too far! What was he trying to do? "Why do you insult me like this?" I asked.

"Because I am your father!" he screamed.

"Well, then, I'll insult you because I am your son."

He hung up on me. Unbelievable! There was our relationship encapsulated in one phone call. Shaking with suppressed fury, I put down the receiver, my fingertips icy. Such a classic Oedipal struggle! I wrote three drafts of a letter to him until I had vented enough anger to strike a conciliatory tone. He was obviously sick, I decided. I should not hold him responsible for his incredible behavior. Then I wrote to the editor of the Madrid newspaper *El País* requesting information from anyone who knew my mother.

"It makes my heart ache to fight with you," I wrote him in that final letter. "Why must we be enemies? Why must we repeat the fate of so many other generations?"

But he never answered, and that phone call must forever remain our last conversation together.

CHAPTER 2: LOSS AND REUNION

MY sister Andrea, now "Sister Benedicta" in an Episcopal order of nuns, and I arrived together at our stepmother Florence's home near Balboa Park. The phone was ringing non-stop. Spain's greatest novelist-in-exile had died, and the Spanish press wanted all the details. Florence, a diminutive, white-haired lady nursing a broken foot, was desolated. Her utter dedication to the man of her dreams had continued in spite of their divorce. To his credit, he had nursed her through several illnesses although he never ceased treating her as a second-class citizen ("Woman! You have just lost a perfect opportunity to keep quiet!"). In his later years, a brief gleam of affection occasionally softened his fierce mockery of her. Also, Florence had learned to stand up for herself against the patriarchal tempests.

After supper we drove to Papá's modern two-bedroom apartment accompanied by Juan, the friend who had found him. It was just the same as always except for the small bloodstain beside the bed where Papá's heart attack had dropped him. Juan explained how, after the coroner's visit, he phoned the funeral society which Papá had joined and they whisked him away.

I glanced at Benedicta. Framed by the black veil and white habit of her order, her elongated Spanish features, dark eyes, strong chin and sensitive mouth, expressed the same strange satisfaction I was feeling. A year and a half apart in ages, our lives remained inextricably intertwined in spite of the different directions we had taken. At last we had access to our father's life without his overwhelming presence. That may seem an unusual sentiment under the circumstances, but he had kept us at such a distance, both from himself and from our Spanish family. Now he was dead, the barriers were gone.

I did not appreciate how many Spanish relatives we had until I opened his address book. Among the names I found our half-brother Emmanuel, whose mother Elizabeth had been our first stepmother in France. Emmanuel at last! Papá did not even admit to his existence until Benedicta wrote a story in which my name was "Manuel" and Julia's was "Elizabeth."

"When Julia read it, she asked me what I remembered," Benedicta said. "That made me smell a rat, and I worked out of her the truth about Elizabeth and Emmanuel as she understood it. Also I used to dream there were three of us children. I had been born one of twins, but the other twin was lost in the war. When I found out about Emmanuel, I stopped having this dream." She leafed through a stack of papers on the coffee table. "Did I ever tell you that I had a compulsion at boarding school to tell what little I knew of the Spain story to anyone who would listen? I would search the dorms for someone who hadn't heard it or, barring that, who might be willing to hear it again. The compulsion stopped after I learned about Emmanuel. I think I must have been searching for someone who could fill in the missing part."

Through the years we repeatedly asked Papá without success for Emmanuel's address. At last here it was, and in Queens, New York! Five minutes later I was talking to him. He spoke English well, but with a French accent. Of course he would fly out for the memorial service.

The downstairs doorbell rang. Margareta, my father's Colombian girlfriend and Florence's nemesis, demanded to see us. She had already made a considerable pest of herself by insisting the funeral society release Papá's body to her for shipment back to Spain— against his express wishes. She must have imagined herself first in the procession of mourners at a state funeral in Madrid. Benedicta would not allow her upstairs so I went down to the lobby.

Another of Papá's loves, a Central American woman poet I had met years earlier, accompanied Margareta. One of his letters to Maurín in the Hoover Library archives described her:

> "My friend is (keep my secret) my lover, my chauffeur, my landlady, my colleague (she writes also and not badly), my housekeeper, and also an enchantress and beautiful (a blonde) and fifteen years younger than I. Not too much, right? To write the enclosed article I had to lock myself in my room (she doesn't leave me in peace for one minute and comes to the door protesting, saying that I'm a thorny type and incivil). And it's not more than ten in the morning after having passed, according to my calculations, fifty hours together! You say that this is delicious? No. It's a sort of chaos with both excellent and exasperating aspects. But that's the way life is!"

I numbered it among my favorite library discoveries because I never had seen this aspect of Papá—flushed with romantic ardor.

Margareta was totally out of control, insulting Florence and claiming to be Papá's only true love. Tearfully she begged for a final viewing of his body. I explained it was impossible. Then she asked me for some of his ashes after the cremation. She had a verbal will on tape, photos of Amparo, paintings, manuscripts. This did not surprise me because Florence and others had described her tendency to trek home from her weekends with him loaded with whatever she could carry. But a verbal will had no legal significance.

Because I hoped to convince her to inventory her memorabilia—and turn over Amparo's photos—I tried to be diplomatic. The conversation continued so long that Benedicta sent the building manager down to make sure Margareta had not added me to her Ramón J. Sender collection. But there had to be some way to pry the photos loose. I would have to visit Margareta and her husband, an extraordinarily understanding and generous man.

Upstairs, I discovered to my relief that Benedicta had opted to sleep in Papá's bed and left me the guest bedroom which he had used as a painting studio. I gave a final lingering glance at the littered desk, the half-corrected proofs on the typing table, the walls covered with his paintings and collages (photos of Brooke Shields figuring strongly in the latter). A copy of Picasso's portrait of Sender as a youth hung over the sofa. When Picasso did not leave him the original in his will, Papá had reproduced it in oils and with complete aplomb signed the famous signature in the corner. On the kitchen table I found my last letter to him, as if he had kept it nearby to reread. My throat ached at this proof of his desire not to forget my offer of a lasting peace, or at least a truce, between us. Well, he had gone to find his lasting peace elsewhere. I could only be grateful I had sent these placating words and not my previous angry drafts.

A few hundred pages of manuscript lay scattered about, the left-hand desk drawer stuffed with forty or so book contracts. Didn't he have a literary agent or a business advisor? On an old tax form I found the name of an accountant and phoned. Yes, Mr. Sender had walked in off the street one day six years earlier. Yes, he had seen Mr. Sender just a few days ago. Papá had said, "I'm through with this business of writing books! Now I'm going to have a good time!" He must have felt his life work was finished.

Page proofs of a manuscript titled *Toque de Queda* lay on his typing table, a collection of brief aphorisms. The Spanish dictionary offered "bugle call for curfew" as a translation, a word which in turn derives from the French for "cover the fire." He wasn't ready for "taps," but I think his literary output had reached a final cadence. After all, he had returned in triumph to Spain and been awarded its top literary prizes. Eighty of his books were in print. Only the Nobel had eluded him. The year he was nominated, he kept insisting he didn't care one way or the other about it. But I knew he was deeply disappointed when another Spaniard was chosen.

Throughout my childhood, he contributed only about a thousand dollars to my expenses and not more than six months of his time. Therefore it came as a complete shock to find bank books crammed with deposits in his desk drawer. The total was more than adequate to support one person off the investment income. The thought of an unexpected windfall was not unattractive. For one thing, it would make Judy's and my planned trip to Spain a great deal easier. The irony was that, if a will did show up, I knew I would be disinherited. Benedicta also felt the same way. She was certain Papá would not have wanted her religious order to benefit from his death.

I mentioned to Benedicta my plans to visit Spain and research Amparo's story in depth. Also I told her of Magdalena's refusal to help. "She said she told you everything during your visit."

She shook her head. "My Spanish was not up to understanding much. I was only there a few days and emotionally the trip was very arduous. I came back very frustrated, with only the sketchiest of details." Her eyebrows puckered. "I didn't send you the notes I took? No? I will when I return."

We visited the mortuary the following day. Both of us wanted to see our father one last time. We could not let him disappear anonymously into the unknown like Amparo. There was Papá, lying on a gurney, a sheet covering him up to the Van Dyke beard on his jutting chin. We gave a sigh of relief, having braced ourselves for something grotesque. He looked like a medieval crusader home from the wars, his bushy eyebrows curving into space over the granite profile. At last we could have our fill of him without the distraction of his gaze.

A first cousin arrived from Barcelona that evening, a tall, bearded man just my age. I was delighted to meet a male blood relative, and we talked until two in the morning. He worked as a journalist for a daily newspaper and was married to an Englishwoman with whom he had two daughters.

In the hopes of shaking loose Margareta's grip on Amparo's letters, I set up an appointment with her in Ensenada and drove down. What could I trade her for Amparo's things? I decided to bring a spoonful of fireplace ashes to masquerade as part of Papá's remains. When I arrived, she took me to her study.

"Do you have the ashes?" she asked.

I handed over the bribe, thinking how amused Papá would have been by this macabre chicanery. She blinked back her tears and with great moans of bereavement tucked the box into her bosom.

"These ashes are our secret," I cautioned her.

"Yes, of course," she replied. "My lips are sealed."

"Now my mother's photos and letters," I said.

"Oh, I'm sorry! I have been so sick with the flu. They are not here!"

She promised to mail them to me. In spite of later phone calls and letters, she never sent them.

"I have a tape I want to play just for you," she whispered. "I think you should hear it."

She turned on the cassette player, and Papá's voice boomed out through the room. He had had a few drinks and was singing Spanish songs in a dulcet baritone. The story he told was the most bizarre he ever concocted. In it he claimed that Amparo and he had broken up early in their relationship and she had returned to Zamora for an abortion. That raised my suspicions. For Amparo with her Catholic convictions to have made such a decision was unimaginable. Besides, her home town of less than twenty thousand people would have been the last place to go for such an operation. My father went on to say that she then had an affair, became pregnant again and came back to Madrid. There she threw herself on his mercy and he magnanimously took her back, promising to accept the child as his own. That was me.

When the lurid tale ended, she paused for my reaction.

"Look, Margareta, as far as I'm concerned I wouldn't mind if he wasn't my father because he was a miserable failure at it." I shrugged. "But every time I look in the mirror I see a Sender."

When I returned to the apartment, the real ashes had arrived during my absence in a cardboard box labeled "Cremains—Ramón J. Sender." I hefted it—about five pounds.

Benedicta had washed the bloodstain out of the carpet and carefully saved the droplets in a bottle. "Take this little bit of him back to Spain with you," she suggested.

I promised her that we would.

Friday night our half-brother Emmanuel arrived. He resembled Papá more than I, the same bullet-shaped head and tendency to baldness. I resembled my paternal grandfather whom my father hated so much that he left home at fourteen. Such a pity Papá had to die to bring about this reunion. Poor man, how many of life's fulfillments he denied himself.

I made sure to get Emmanuel's mother's address because I wanted to visit her in France. After all, she had been our surrogate mother for a year or more. Only circumstances had prevented us from growing up with her. He described his childhood: Papá's abandonment of them had been total. They had survived the siege of Barcelona and barely avoided the French internment camps where so many Spaniards died. Later he was shunted from boarding schools to relatives and back.

Although Papá always had insisted he never had married Elizabeth, Emmanuel explained they were wed in a civil ceremony. Papá always had disparaged Elizabeth, saying he returned home from a trip to find her mistreating us. That same day he had taken us away and never saw her again. I was eager to hear Elizabeth's version and find out what memories, if any, her face would evoke.

Eight days after Papá's death, we boarded a motorized sloop to scatter his ashes in the Pacific Ocean. A TV crew affiliated with Madrid television accompanied us. Benedicta handed the box to Florence who wanted to be the one to empty it over the side. Florence's broken foot made it difficult for her to turn around so, in actuality, it was I who upended the silvered cardboard container. As the sea wind spattered salt spray in my face, the last traces of my father drifted away.

But I had miscalculated the pitch of the boat and a handful of bone fragments landed on deck. When I scooped them overboard, I palmed four or five. These I would carry to Spain with me, to Amparo. The bottle of Papá's blood Benedicta washed out of the carpet I would place somewhere appropriate in Aragon, his birthplace.

My obsession with Amparo's story intensified, underscored by the many responses I received to my printed letter in Madrid's *El País*. Also I received the notes my sister had written during her trip to Spain. They offered surprising revelations about Amparo's death as well as new mysteries. She had learned that when the civil war began in July, 1936, our parents were spending the summer with us at a rustic chalet on the outskirts of San Rafael, a mountain resort north of Madrid. I was twenty-one months old, Andrea eight months. Papá, so the story went, had gone to Madrid on some errand. While he was there, the battle lines closed and Amparo could not reach him, nor he her. Confused, she returned to Zamora, her family home. En route she tried to phone Papá, but was arrested as a spy and detained a week. During the separation, I became inconsolably upset. Amparo was released, only to be arrested again a few weeks later in Zamora. Andrea remained with her in prison. When it became known that Amparo was going to be killed, relatives tried hard to prevent it, but the danger to them was great.

Amparo had been shot on October eleventh, 1936, by a certain Segundo Viloria. Amparo's two brothers had been shot some weeks earlier and their bodies were never recovered. Six years later, seventeen-year-old Magdalena disinterred our mother's body from her unmarked grave in spite of people who threatened her and called her "a Red." She had placed Amparo in the family mausoleum, but her name was not inscribed on the stone until after Franco's death in 1975 because it was not safe.

The notes also revealed my sister's tears and torment. I understood why she had never sent them to me earlier. Rather than answering my questions, they only increased my need to learn the whole story. But now, at least, I knew the name of my mother's killer.

O N our trip to Spain, I realized how the film of my life was running in reverse, unpeeling the layers: Paris, from where we departed for America in 1939, Calais, where my sister had almost died of pneumonia in a refugee children's camp during the winter of 1938. And then Biarritz, where the Red Cross reunited us with our father in late 1937 and where I now crossed the frontier to stand once more upon Spanish soil. Finally to Madrid, my birthplace. At last I understood why it had taken me so long to come back. My father's vow not to return during Franco's reign and his warnings about my safety were partial reasons, but the most important reason of all was that throughout my life, "Spain" had named the wound in my psyche.

In Madrid, an elfin grandmother opened the door of my cousin Ana María's apartment. She was my Aunt Conchita, my father's older sister, eighty-five years old and still going strong. Her deeply set eyes sparkled from under a prominent brow, her blunt nose seemed an exact copy of my father's. What incredible luck! Of all the Sender relatives, she had known Amparo best.

"I'm living here now with Ana María," Conchita explained. "The doctor has given me a new asthma medicine which keeps me well."

She gave me a loving smile. "Ohhh, Monchín! It's been so long!" Her gnarled hand grasped mine, that same hand which had held me as a baby.

Her voice seemed so familiar! I had no trouble understanding her dramatic inflections and emotional turns of phrase.

"I haven't seen you in so many years! Yet, without seeing you, I have seen you grow up." She leaned against my leg, stroking my thigh. "I always asked myself—" She closed her eyes and her voice softened. "'How are they at this moment?' Also, I knew your American foster mother Julia. I met her and her husband here in Madrid before the War."

"No, it couldn't have been Julia," I replied. "She has never been to Spain."

"Yes, yes, Julia Davis." Conchita insisted. "They knew your father here. They lived in Conn-ect-ee-coot." She pronounced the word in a marvelous Castilian.

"But they can't be the same people you met here!"

"I knew her." Conchita did not give up her opinions easily.

"But—"

"Grandma," her granddaughter interjected from across the room. "Ramón says that the woman you met here was not the one who took care—she used the verb *amparar* (Amparo), meaning to protect or to shelter—of them."

Conchita snorted. "Well, perhaps since I had met this other couple already, your father thought, 'Because Conchita knows these people, I'll give her this version.'"

Obviously she was aware of my father's tendency to bend the truth to his purposes. I waited until Conchita and I were alone in the room. "Now tell me about the beginning of the War," I coaxed. I had already learned that in Spain "the War" always referred to the Civil War.

She settled herself more comfortably on the sofa. "Well, for some years we had rented a villa in the summer colony of San Rafael— even before your parents met." She glanced at me. "Do you know it? No? It's northwest of Madrid in the Guadarrama Mountains, situated on both sides of La Coruña highway which runs all the way to Galicia. The air is fresh there and the velvet green forests climb up to the sky. We always rented the same chalet, Villa Frutos, the last one on the road toward Avila. Behind it the valley descends through meadows to the river. The ravines are full of blackberries and tangles of ivy and creepers. But in 1936 Emi, my husband, had suffered stomach problems all winter and was on a special diet. We decided to stay in Madrid that summer and not go to San Rafael. Our children had gone to the Pyrenees with their grandfather to get out of the heat. Meanwhile, your father Pepe, that was his family nickname, rented Villa Frutos in Emi's name to retain his anonymity. He left with Amparo and you children as well as the servant girls.

"A few days later Emi said, 'We're going to San Rafael.'

"I said, 'Don't tell me stupidities.'

"'Well, I've just been posted to San Rafael for twenty-five days,' he said. He worked for the telegraph company. 'We have a travel allowance to pay for a hotel. Won't Pepe and Amparo be surprised!'

"So off we went, four days before the Civil War started." She snapped open her fan and wafted air in my direction. Its winglike movements punctuated all our conversations. "The Hotel Golf, where we took a room, was face-to-face with the telephone office. It was there we heard the news that rightists in Madrid had murdered a popular lieutenant of the assault guards. This force was created by the Republic to function as a trustworthy city police as opposed to the civil guard who were of doubtful loyalty. The lieutenant's friends avenged him by shooting the Monarchist leader Calvo Sotelo. These events immediately were followed on July 18th by military uprisings in Morocco and many cities.

"That day we came to the chalet for lunch with your parents. When we arrived, Amparo was seated in the shade of the chestnut tree in the front yard with Andrea asleep beside her in a wicker basket covered with cheesecloth. During the meal, we listened to the radio. The Burgos station was in the hands of the rebels and reported that General Mola had sent troops into the streets of Pamplona. Other generals had taken Valladolid, Zaragoza, Cádiz, and Córdoba.

"'General Franco has declared the constitution worthless,' the announcer said. 'The army can no longer stand idly by and is rising to bring justice, equality and peace to all Spaniards.'

"Meanwhile, Madrid radio insisted that no one on the mainland had taken part in 'the absurd plot.' But Pepe insisted the situation was very grave and the rebellion widespread.

"'The press called for the demobilization of the army a week ago, but the ministers just whine for law and order,' he grumbled. 'Now the workers are screaming for arms but the government is afraid to distribute them!'

"'Will we be safe here?' Amparo asked.

"You see, San Rafael was a rightist enclave," Conchita explained. "That morning two cars were parked in front of the President of the Council's villa with six police in each, all armed with machine guns. Unpleasant types. And if a general mobilization began, Pepe would have to fight. The Alto de León pass between us and Madrid had to be defended.

"'Amparo, you remain here with Conchita,' he told her. 'Emi has no political reputation and will not be in danger. If things get worse, take the children to your family in Zamora. From there it's only a half-hour to Portugal where you can find passage to France.'

Conchita frowned. "All through that night we lived beside the radio! A rightist general captured Seville and Franco flew to Morocco to assume command of the troops. Sunday at dawn, two announcements prompted Pepe to act—the requisition of all private cars by the workers, which meant a general mobilization, and the arming of all the Popular Front organizations. He left to phone Segovia and place himself under orders of the provincial government. When he returned, he reported Segovia in the hands of the fascists and a confused atmosphere in San Rafael. The civil guards had disappeared from their barracks and armed workers were patrolling the streets.

"Franco himself broadcast a speech from Spanish Morocco: 'I hereby proclaim that the army must respond to the wishes of the majority,' he said. He went on to declare martial law. Obviously it meant civil war. All that night and Monday the 20th we remained in suspense. The fighting in Madrid favored the workers and the rebel general Goded's surrender speech in Barcelona raised their enthusiasm to a peak. Then at five that evening in the hotel we heard a commotion. We were taking a siesta, and Emi left the room whistling to investigate.

"'What's going on?' he asked a bellhop.

"'Civil guards are standing with fixed bayonets in front of the telephone office! You cannot go outside. Everyone's in the foyer with the doors locked!'

"He had not finished speaking when—rat-tat-tat-tat-tat!— machine-gun fire erupted. Everyone was terrified! A half-hour later, the hotel manager went out on the street. Several telephone employees who had tried to escape lay dead on the sidewalk and others were dead inside the building. Someone said, 'They cut all the phone lines and didn't leave one person alive!'" Conchita's eyes darkened. "Ah, what horrors! What were they trying to do? The telegraph office was only some one hundred meters further and Emi was scheduled for duty the following morning!

"'You're not going,' I said.

"'I have to," he said. 'After all, I'm commissioned to this service. Those of us in charge have to be there in case something happens.'

"'Why are you going to search out a bullet?' I asked.

"We were arguing like this when your father appeared in his pajamas and slippers. 'I've come to tell you to leave everything in the hotel and come to our house,' he said. 'They won't shoot at us there because it's an isolated place. Here you're in the center of town!'

"Emi replied, 'I can't, because the moment we're in a declared war I'm under military orders. I have to stay here.'

"'Not me!' I said. And I went with Pepe.

My father gave an eye-witness report of this incident in his book *Counterattack in Spain*. A truck of civil guards, rural police hostile to the workers and leftists, had returned to San Rafael. When they were hailed by a squad of militiamen, they opened fire. Everyone took cover except one youth who stood in front of the truck, hands on his hips.

"What you have done is a cowardly crime!" he shouted.

The officer in the truck leaped to the pavement and shouted hysterical orders. "He's their leader! Cover the crowd! Leave him to me!"

But no one was in sight. They had disappeared into nearby houses. Pistol in the youth's back, the officer forced him into the entrance of the telephone exchange and fired two shots into him. The civil guards entered the building shooting, collected their families from the barracks and drove off towards Segovia again.

"*Díos mío*, when Pepe told us this, we were terrified! What were we to do? I was convinced I would never see Emi again!"

Early the following day, Victor Rivera arrived with his wife and their two little girls Maruchi and Pepi. As Director-General of Mountains, a post equivalent to being the head of the U.S. Forest Service, he had the forestry residence at his disposal, a short distance from the center of town. Although Amparo had just met them that year, they were old friends of Papá, Conchita and Emi. They had come by way of the river behind the town, Victor in an old jacket, his wife in a cook's apron.

"Ten forestry guards surrounded our house armed to the teeth!" Victor told them. "I dared to ask the sergeant who had given the order. 'Sir, the military governor of Segovia,' he said. I decided we shouldn't stay longer because the second order would be to shoot us. So we left casually with our two servant women and tried to get into the hotel. The manager refused us rooms but agreed to put up the servants. We continued here by way of the river. Pepe, we should get out. A busload of armed fascist youth have arrived from Valladolid. They'll stir up trouble."

Rivera and my father began to plan to leave San Rafael because both were known government sympathizers. But the road over the Sierras was unsafe. There were armed men everywhere.

"Santiago will get us out of here," Papá said.

Santiago was a retired shepherd who knew the mountains well. When he wasn't working for the family, he ran errands for the sanitarium down the road. But who would go there to find him?

"Look, I'll do it," Conchita said. "I'll take those milk crocks, wear a servant's apron and walk over. If anyone asks, I'll say, 'My master has children and I always come to buy milk at the sanitarium early in the morning.' If I have a dumb expression, they'll let me pass!"

The sanitarium had one hundred beds for children. A dairy on the premises provided milk for them and the surplus was sold. Before anyone could argue, Conchita left. She stayed off the road as much as possible and had no trouble. The lack of traffic seemed ominous and oppressive. It was a stifling day which promised a thunderstorm. At the sanitarium, they told her that Santiago had gone to El Espinar with a truck but would return soon. She waited until he arrived.

"Santiago, you have to take my brother and another man across the mountain any way you can," she said.

"Nothing doing!" he said. "Terrible things are happening! They'll shoot at us! I'm not going up there. Every time I do I get in trouble!"

But Conchita finally changed Santiago's mind.

"All right, I'll do what you say," he said. "Tell them to wear casual clothes and carry a newspaper or a sack. They should look as if they are out for a stroll to collect pine cones. I'll wait for them by the forest behind the meadow."

She returned to the chalet and reported to the men before joining

Amparo and the children in the backyard. Pepi, the Riveras' young-est daughter, was a blonde butterball who liked to mother me and Andreina. Amparo was distraught over the situation. She wanted to accompany Papá, but the children never could have walked over the mountain.

That evening the Riveras' servants, Celes the cook and Adelina the nursemaid, arrived with alarming news.

"The fascist militia are searching for *Señor* Rivera everywhere!" they said. "Also they want *Señor* Sender, but they think he's the secretary of some ministry or other."

Papá laughed, flattered to be given such a dignified post. Celes and Adelina insisted on staying because of the unsettled situation in town. Everyone ate supper beside the blaring radio.

What happened that night in Villa Frutos can be surmised from my father's novel *The Five Books of Ariadne*. Here Ariadne speaks for Amparo, Javier for my father. The autobiographical parallels, Conchita assured me, are unmistakable.

> "That night Javier (Ramón) and I stayed awake. I asked him if he loved me. He looked at me out of the corners of his eyes and smiled without replying, as if to say, 'To a silly question, an intelligent silence.' All the same, he knew I enjoyed his silences. I adored him. He was every-thing that I wasn't. . . . I don't know how to explain it, be-cause the best things of love never have had nor will have any explanation. . . .
>
> "I began to cry without knowing why—sometimes love oversensitizes me. Javier looked at me smiling.
>
> "'How can you laugh watching me cry?' I asked him.
>
> "'Your weeping only means that you have touched the pinnacle of joy,' he replied.
>
> "'And where have you learned so much, Professor?' I teased.
>
> "Javier removed a paper from a notebook. He read a sonnet which he said was by Aldana (famous for his love poems, and nicknamed "El Divino" by Cervantes) in the times of King Carlos V:
>
> > "What is the reason, Ariadne, that here
> > clasped in the maelstrom of love,
> > tongues, arms and feet entwined,

a vine laced amongst the jasmine
whose vital breath we sip together,
that now and then we are forced
to cry and gasp
through kiss-surfeited lips?

My love, my lovely Ariadne, inside
our joined souls you call our bodies to unite
again within this furnace.
Yet as water in a sponge cannot pass
from soul to the sweet center,
the mortal shell decries its miserly luck.

"It surprised me to discover that what had happened
to me also happened to women in the time of Carlos V . . .
I thanked him, because he had changed the name of the
beloved from Phyllis to Ariadne. . . .
'"Well, I'm going," he said at last.'

Conchita remembered how the household awakened before dawn.
The radio reported that rebel soldiers had fired machine guns into
strolling crowds in Salamanca. Assault guards had captured the socialist leaders of Valladolid. Huelva and Granada were taken but
Madrid remained free. And Barcelona, that citadel of radicalism, as
well. Pepe and the Riveras were drinking hot coffee in the kitchen
when Amparo joined them with Andreina in her arms. Pepe zipped
up his leather jacket and kissed Andreina's plump cheek. As a going-
away memento, Amparo gave him a small photo of herself with an
inscription on the back.

"Amparo, be cautious," he warned. "You must burn anything
with my name on it including my manuscripts."

"But some are your only copies!" she protested.

"Nothing must show I was living here with you." He kissed her
on the cheek. "Now I must go. Walk with me to the edge of the
woods."

"I'm going with Victor," his wife announced. "His health is poor
and I don't want to be separated. Conchita, will you be responsible
for the girls and servants?"

"Don't worry," Conchita assured her. "I will treat them the same
as my niece and nephew."

"Put on your heaviest shoes," Papá told Victor's wife. "And don't
carry anything." He held up his binoculars. "This is all I'm taking."

He repeated his warning to Conchita. "Burn anything that might define the household as leftist—books, papers. There's a good chance the place will be searched. Above all, do nothing to draw suspicion on yourselves."

In *The Five Books of Ariadne*, Ariadne tells what happened next:

> "We left . . . Javier asked me to accompany him not only to give the innocent impression of a married couple but also because he had something to tell me. Something important. What? I didn't know. The truth is that he didn't tell me . . . I had one of those moments of inhibition from which I sometimes suffer. I was waiting for him to cross over the silence to me. We walked without speaking. We approached the woods. Near us there was a tree struck by lightning. . . .
>
> "'I'm going on my way without kissing you because I don't wish to call attention to us,' he said. 'I know your kiss is worth some risk, but I don't want that risk to be yours. It may seem no one is around, but a man with binoculars could be watching us from somewhere nearby.' . . .
>
> "He entered the woods slowly. All at once I lost sight of him. He left at the exact instant he should have left. An hour earlier it would have been difficult and two hours later impossible . . . I could not remember his saying goodbye, either in the house or outside . . . I went on thinking that we had separated only for a few days, nothing more . . . The rent had been paid until September. That thought, so ridiculous under the circumstances, somehow comforted me."

Amparo met the Riveras on their way out the gate. Victor carried a camera, and they were chatting quietly to give the impression of a casual tourist couple. A half-hour later, the women heard the distant roar of motors. A convoy of trucks with cannon approached. The troops were the rebel Colonel Serrador's column of two thousand soldiers on their way south to attack Madrid.

Conchita: "The last words I heard Pepe speak to Amparo were, 'Remember, if worst comes to worst, go to Zamora. Nothing ever happens in Zamora.' If only it had been true!"

Once more I realized how Zamora held the final clue to Amparo's fate.

A PROVINCIAL
CHILDHOOD

"THE most loyal and noble city of Zamora," the
fifteenth-century king Enrique IV dubbed in
perpetuity this fortified town on the banks
of the Duero River. The rocky escarpments have been inhabited
since ancient times. Its castles protected the roads from Portugal to
the west and Galicia to the north. The city banner was decorated
with eight red streamers for the eight battles won against the Ro-
mans. From the repeated conquests by and defeats of the Moors
evolved the popular saying, "Zamora is not won in an hour." Ferdi-
nand the Great added an emerald ribbon in recognition of the city's
help in the final battle that united Spain. Although the twelfth-cen-
tury cathedral was capped by an unusual Serbio-Byzantine dome of
feathery overlapping stones, the town did not attract many tourists.
Except for Holy Week, when over forty different religious groups
marched in the procession, foreigners usually preferred the elegant
architecture of the medieval university town Salamanca to the
south.

In *The Five Books of Ariadne,* Ariadne tells how she grew up in
the shadow of the cathedral. In Amparo's case, it was actually the
Church of San Juan on the Plaza Major, a half-block away from her

35

family's Café Iberia. The shadow widened in the morning and then diminished little by little all day long. When the townhall clock struck the hours, the children marked the edges of the shadow on the paving stones with a nail. That way, when the clock was broken, they could calculate the time from their sun dial.

Ariadne's memories of those years were luminous, days full of light and magical nights. Their house had an attic which the children transformed in their games into a castle or a pirate ship.

Amparo's father Antonio married twice. His first wife bore three children, Saturnino, Casimira and Magdalena. When she died, Antonio married Amparo's mother, a young woman from the local village of Perdigon who was serving as a maid in the household. She gave birth to Nati who suffered from nervous problems, Amparo, Antonio and Eugenia. This second wife died in childbirth when Amparo was seven.

Among the many children, Amparo's older sister Casimira would play a prominent role in determining her fate. Casimira was the scholar of the family. She had studied in France for some years before returning and marrying a man named Miguel Sevilla. He was an ecclesiastical tailor and a leader of the conservative Carlist *requetés*, the paramilitary groups named after a reactionary nineteenth-century pretender to the throne. His name would recur frequently in explanations of my mother's death. Indeed, my father in his novel *The Affable Hangman* chose the name 'Sevilla' for a criminal condemned to die by the garrote. There he described the man's final agony in gruesome detail, extracting the vengeance otherwise denied him.

Amparo kept fond memories of her childhood in Zamora. In his fiction, my father recounted Ariadne's earliest recollection—the smell of tobacco on her father's left hand.

> "Everyone treated me as if I were a perfect being, my parents, the household, my neighbors. However I was a little animal, greedy and full of desires, always sniffing the air for colors and superficial pleasures. I owned a piece of white silk over which I would pass my hand and put it to my lips and cheeks . . . I didn't have the slightest idea of men. I thought of them as a large and hairy hand which smelled in a rare manner and one day would entrap and overtake me and carry me to another house and give me

money. After this, I would get fat and give birth to a baby boy, but of this last item it was better not to speak . . .

"I remember other strange things of that time. (When I came in dirty from playing in the street,) my aunt would say, 'These people are not from your sphere, child.' I began to believe I lived inside a crystal ball tinted the lightest blue. Outside it the wolves howled, the adults cried and the guards hung the thieves . . . I became accustomed to the idea that I was pretty. I remember that, when alone, I thought: 'Well, everyone wants to kiss me, but what's in it for me?'

"My father had his office on a central street . . . 'Why do you go to the office so much?' I asked him.

"'To earn money, child, to buy you clothes and toys,' our cook replied.

"After that, whenever I went to his office and saw some bills or coins on the table—change from something he had sent out to buy—I thought, 'This is all he has earned so far today, but later there will be more.' There was something about the earning of money that seemed miraculous and incomprehensible but which was related to the smell of his hand. If I saw no money on the table, I became sad and thought, 'Poor Papá!'

"On election days I heard people speak about whether they had voted. The expression 'vote' sounded like 'bote' to me and to us children this word meant a ball game. We would throw a ball into the sky and measure how high it bounced. 'My ball bounced higher than yours,' we would say, and try to prove it. There were no classes on election days because the schools were used as polling places.

"'Today the school is full of "boting" people,' I said to my father. I imagined the adults throwing balls and jumping about like cats and billy goats. 'What for?'

"'Well, daughter, to elect deputies,' he replied. 'This is a democracy.'

"For many years, democracy meant to me a group of men leaping together like young bulls. No one ever cared to explain these errors to me . . . But my most persistent memory is of my first communion. I kneeled in my beautiful dress, and from the instant I took the wafer on my tongue, I believed myself semidivine. Yet suddenly I had to urinate. To be lifted up bodily to God to go to the bathroom was a horrible thought . . ."

In 1912, Amparo's father opened the Café Iberia and moved the family from a house on the square to the apartment above the cafe. As a nonbelligerent nation during World War I, Spain grew prosperous selling food and clothing to both sides. Improved communications brought new ideas that echoed through Zamora's wine shops and cobblestoned alleys. Communism, anarchism and socialism were debated fiercely in the Barayón cafe. For Amparo as a child, it was an important political awakening.

Feliza, a tiny woman who was Amparo's best childhood friend, lived in an apartment full of antique furnishings including a three-story dollhouse taller than she with a clock on its cupola.

"Amparo and I were intimate friends because I lived in Number 1 and she in Number 3," she chirped in a voice that mingled with the canary in the other room. "Her father would place a few café tables on the street near his parrot which insulted anyone who walked by his perch. My father and I would sit there to drink coffee. Amparo would join us because she was a great chatterer. We were very animated and laughed like rattlebrains at anything anyone said to us. All the Barayóns were great *cafeteros* and Amparo was no exception. She loved to talk. I began to stay with her and we became great, great friends. We used to go riding at my family's ranch, Amparo on a horse and me on a burro, just like Don Quixote and Sancho Panza."

One Friday during Lent, rabbit was served for lunch at the Barayóns. Magdalena, Amparo's older half-sister, stared at it and said, "*Andaaa!* What can we do? We can't eat meat!"

And Amparo replied, "Look, we can't waste it!" She stood up and raised her hand in a blessing. "I now baptize you 'fish!'"

Amparo attended a one-room school for girls run by three single sisters across the back alley from the café. In a class photo, she stands in the back row, her full lips visible above the fan she is holding, dark eyes dramatic and mischievous. She must have been eleven or twelve years old. How could this lovable child later be betrayed by those who had smiled at her girlish pranks?

In *The Five Books of Ariadne* I glimpsed more details:

> "I had a tutor, María Jesús. She was only three years older than I and although she was my teacher, in a certain sense I educated her. I had ideas, good or bad. She, no. She only knew what she had learned in books and could not

think for herself. I never saw anything suggestive in her behavior, but at times the large size of her bosoms made me squirm.

"My father (as a widower) courted her. The day she told me about my father's feelings for her, I felt in her voice something new and suspicious. She talked with great seriousness and without ridiculing my father's pretensions. There was in her remarks a cynical reserve I did not like.

"'Marry whomever you like, but don't play at being odalisques,' I told her.

"María Jesus was similar to me and my friends in that she loved people with a complete unawareness of sex. Between parentheses, I have always believed that this sexless love, in which one sees the beloved in a cloud, in a flower or feels his absence as that of God himself, is the unique dignity human love contains. The rest is just localized desires, like hunger and thirst.

"I observed that my father's advances scared María Jesús. Along with her I felt a mixture of gratitude, repugnance and curiosity. I watched her and thought, 'She has too much bosom, and because of this she is poised to place herself in those male hands that smell of tobacco, that want to devour and possess her completely.'

"She noticed that her reaction to my father was not what I had expected . . . One day she said, 'You want me to ridicule your father's advances, but I can't. Just look at what he wrote me yesterday.'

"In the note he told her he was in love with her and could not imagine being old and renouncing life. For him, life was María Jesús. He also said he would only act the part of man and wife with her for one or two years before dying. My father's capacity for love seemed to be the same as in his youth, but naturally to indulge in excesses at his age would have been extremely dangerous. He told her it didn't matter to him if he died after the honeymoon. Furthermore he added slyly that what little money he had would be hers on the day of his death.

"María Jesús looked very serious and repeated, 'How can I make fun of a man like this?'

"To call my father 'a man' made me uncomfortable. It sounded a little indecent . . .

"We children classified women in several ways. There were odalisques, houris and other Moslem types. Once my friend Carmen asked what an odalisque was.

"'It's obvious,' I replied. 'It's a depilated, undulating, perfumed woman who calls her fiancé "my promised one" and refers to getting married as "changing one's condition." When the fiancé is presented to her family, he has "formalized relations" and calls marriage "that sweet yoke" and pregnancy "an interesting state."'

"I would not have dared to say 'pregnancy' in the full light, but the room was dark. The boys held their solemn assemblies apart from us girls, and hid some of their slang expressions out of respect. Nevertheless one or two filtered through. We knew that a girl who watched and protected her virginity, but was passed compliantly hand-to-hand to successive boyfriends, was called a 'virgin-harlot.'"

In 1917, when a national strike was savagely repressed, the local Communist Party gained many new members. The following year, the famous influenza epidemic killed many, including Amparo's father. She imagined that, as an orphan, she would go to live with the nuns. The idea evoked in her a bittersweet emotion, but she remained in the family apartment under the care of her half-sister Magdalena. Amparo's half-brother Saturnino took over the operation of the family café and the ice factory several blocks away.

The younger children sang a ditty about Magdalena:

"Magdalena is very ugly
And has a terrible voice
She doesn't know how to cook
And has an atrocious temper."

Amparo herself had a temper. According to her sister Eugenia, she could be treacherous. "She would take a glass and say that if we children continued fighting she'd break it. She would throw it. We all laughed so much!"

When she was twelve, Amparo began to study piano, first with her half-sister Casimira and then with a Señora Muñoz. After taking communion at eight o'clock Mass, she would eat breakfast and then practice until lunchtime. In the early afternoon she came downstairs to wait on customers. Often she was asked to play piano in the café. Later she returned to the apartment to practice again. People would come out on their balconies to listen.

She liked to work in the café and talk to people because something amusing was always happening. The men who gambled at roulette and baccarat in a side room hired her as their lookout. Many pesetas changed hands while Amparo kept an eye peeled for the police. If they arrived, she gave the signal and the men escaped through the alley. When fights occurred, Amparo separated the combatants.

The Five Books of Ariadne depicts this period:

> "At thirteen I saw and heard people talking about me
> in roundabout ways. Well, I did not believe there was any-
> thing in life that was ugly or should be prohibited. Our
> bodies functioned like perfect machines and our souls as
> well. When I loved someone, it was certain he or she
> would not lose a moment to love me back. Colors were for
> my eyes, the breezes to cool my temples. Always I hoped
> for something, but I did not know what. True, in the street
> I saw ugly men and women—much too ugly! But I be-
> lieved they would be able to overcome their ugliness some
> day. The King and the Pope were to blame for ugly people
> and social injustices, and I supposed that by devotion and
> difficult heroic acts, the sort one reads in children's sto-
> ries, something would be done to cure them."

Ariadne tells of an old curate in the neighborhood who had an absolute horror of flies. So much so that he never opened his garret window except at night. The older boys used to go out and trap flies by the hundreds in a sack, using a few pieces of licorice as bait. After dark, they would sneak up under the old man's window where he was hunched over his prayerbook beside the lamp. They opened the sack and the light attracted the flies. Up they rose like smoke right into his room, while he called upon Mary and the Saints.

The lack of a mother during her teens allowed Amparo more freedom than was usual in those times, and she developed into a very independent teenager. The café provided her with a stage, an opportunity to mix with the townspeople who obviously loved her. It served as a meeting place for liberals whose opinions of a modern woman's role helped shape this unusual adolescent's view of what her life should be. The magnetic poles of her existence were San Juan's, a mere hundred yards away, and Café Iberia. Within these environs, she grew into a flamboyant young adult. But she drank a lot of coffee, and her liveliness contained a nervous edge. Her fingers sometimes trembled.

Her best friend Feliza remembered the musical-literary parties they held as teenagers. "We all smoked, something extremely rare in Zamora. We were too shy to buy the cigarettes ourselves but asked a boyfriend or else Amparo sent a waiter. Absolutely shameless! Amparo would play piano, someone would recite verses, another would read an essay. If someone had written something, they would read it. Another would sing. This way we passed our time together.

"There was also a popular tango she sang—'Smoking, I wait for the man I love . . .'" She began to sing:

> "Smoking I wait
> For the man I love
> Behind the panes
> Of the bright windows
> And meanwhile I smoke
> So that I don't fret my life away."

"Her eyes were a little sad. They always showed her moods, but she could laugh too.

"In the early 1920s she used to write articles and drama reviews for *El Mercantíl* and *El Heraldo De Zamora*. She signed them 'Miguelina Ascona,' because her full name was Amparo Barayón Miguel Ascona. She was very considerate. Poor people would come asking for *la señorita niña* to beg for alms. She would always give them something."

In 1923, a cultural club modelled on Madrid's Ateneo began to meet at the Café Iberia. Amparo was among its founding members.

"She had a good friend, a Professor Bientobas at the University of Salamanca. He wasn't a boyfriend, but would come to chat with her because she was a tremendous conversationalist. She loved to talk about everything—literature, music." Feliza smiled wistfully. "*Ai*, those marvelous long summer afternoons with picnics on the knoll!"

Feliza stressed an important point: "I also want to say that Amparo was Catholic from top to bottom! From daily Mass to daily communion, Amparo was the parish priest's right hand. We children sang the Flowers of May, a devotion to the Virgin during the whole month with many canticles about the flowers. Amparo played the harmonium and conducted us. The last day of the Novena of Flowers, we came down from the choir loft to the sacristy and were given little cakes. She taught catechism and prepared children for first communion. In those days, catechism teachers were greatly respected. When the children saw her in the street, they ran up and kissed her. She gave them caramels and little religious cards which she signed at the bottom: 'Live for your friend, Amparito Barayón.'"

Of the many songs the children sang, one included the following verse and refrain:

> "A thousand beautiful cherubs
> Form your canopy.
> I want to be with them.
> Virgin, take me with you to heaven.
> My longing will be crowned!
> How happy I shall be!
>
> Take our hearts,
> Pure Virgin.
> Do not abandon us,
> Ever, ever, ever."

Her first serious romance occurred when she was twenty-three, the same year she went to Madrid for the first time and passed her piano examinations with honors. His name was Aguirre, a sergeant in the army from Salamanca. He wrote articles for the newspapers, and she liked him because of this. They went to morning Mass together often and then in the evening to say the rosary, which was unusual because normally only women attended the rosary. It was the act of a man very much in love. Then one day a young lady from Salamanca appeared, obviously his hometown sweetheart. Through a go-between she asked to speak to Amparo.

"The girl arrived at our house with a neighbor," Amparo's younger sister Eugenia reported. "We decided to put on a show for her. I dressed up as a maid to open the door, but I had to hide because the neighbor knew me. I was going to bring a tray with her visiting card. So the daughter of the cook—Andrés the waiter's sister—opened the door and interviewed her. She brought her into the salon where Amparo was playing the piano to make a good impression. They began to talk and the girl claimed Aguirre was returning to her."

"'I don't want him to spend time with you because I love him with all my soul,' she told Amparo. 'Tell him you don't want him.'

"'If it's only because you love him and there isn't anything more serious between you—well, then, I love him too!' Amparo replied.

"They said goodbye. When Aguirre called on Amparo later, he slunk into the room, very ashamed that this young woman had visited her. Amparo told him that as far as she was concerned he was free to choose between them. So he continued seeing her, but she no longer trusted him. He hadn't told her the truth. Also, the other woman stayed on in Zamora until he finished his military service—he had only a little time left. But he kept going to daily Mass and the rosary with Amparo, while the other saw him at the barracks. This other woman had some sort of hold on him because she had met his family.

"Amparo tried to remain detached. When he completed his tour of duty, he returned to Salamanca. A newspaper reporter was a friend of Amparo's. She paid him to go to Salamanca and check on Aguirre. She wanted to know where he went and with whom. He returned to Zamora and said Aguirre was spending time with the other woman. They were together morning and evening, but at the same time he was writing Amparo every day and she was answering him. So Amparo returned all his letters to him with a note telling him to go with God and asked him to mail her letters back. He returned her letters and photos with a reply: 'To the woman whom I loved, these photos which I liked so much. Vanity of vanities!'"

After the relationship with Aguirre ended, Amparo took a civil service placement exam in Salamanca. But the job was given to a widow with two children, a native of the city. Amparo was ambitious, however, and preferred teaching piano and catechism to housework, sewing or cooking. Next she took the telephone exam in Zamora in which she placed first. So she began to work long hours for the phone company, but continued behind the café's register for a few hours each day.

Her job required her to visit people in their homes and convince them to install a telephone. The idea of a woman working in sales was something unusual for provincial Zamora, and shocking to the older set. By then she had cut her hair and was wearing cloche hats, Zamora's first flapper.

She must have demonstrated considerable talent at her work, because she was soon offered a transfer to Madrid. For Amparo, it was a dream come true, a way to escape the confines of her isolated birthplace.

"I saw Amparo only once, when I was seventeen and my father died," Eugenia's husband, a retired civil guard, reported. "She was friendly with my father. All the civil guards of Zamora went to drink coffee at the Café Iberia. Amparo held conversations with all the clients. When she heard my father had died, she came to the barracks to offer her condolences, and this was the only time I saw her. When I began a relationship with your aunt, Amparo had already gone to Madrid. She must have left for Madrid in 1930."

So at twenty-six, she took the train to the capital, leaving a scandalized family behind. A single woman striking out on her own in the big city? Shocking! Of course Casimira had travelled to France to attend the university, but she returned home to marry within the Church. Now she shared the view of the other female relatives who were convinced Amparo was travelling to her ruination, if not damnation as well. Six years later, Casimira would see to it that her prophesy of doom would be fulfilled.

CHAPTER 5: A LIFE IN MADRID,
1930—1934

I N January 1930, the dictator Primo de Rivera
had resigned and gone into exile. He had
been vilified by everyone including the mili-
tary and the press, and especially by the students whom he himself
had hated the most. Some years earlier he had jailed my father. A
rebellion had broken out at the artillery academy in Segovia. Although journalists had been prohibited to enter the city, Papá decided to sneak in. He dressed in the smock and visored cap of a
sidewalk photographer and took a camera on a tripod. In that dis-
guise, he had no trouble entering the city. Once inside, friends told
him everything about the artillerymen's revolt. His published articles alerted the government, and someone identified him as Sender.
They wanted him, dead or alive. When they found him, they locked
him up in Modelo Prison. But the public outcry was so loud they
had to release him after three months.

When Amparo arrived in Madrid, she found the streets buzzing
with talk about how Spain was on the eve of the millennium. The
socialist leader Besteiro's manifesto calling for the reestablishment
of the Republic had been distributed clandestinely, and the Socialists were the best organized party in the nation. How exciting to be

living in this marvelous city with its broad avenues, to be a part of this epoch-making time! She revelled in her new-found emancipation from Zamora's provincialism, especially from Saturnino who overplayed his role as head of the household.

During the next months she would cast off the bourgeois restraints of her upbringing and become a freethinker. Away from the scrutiny of her family, she was free to embrace a feminist perspective, even to live openly with a man and to bear his child out of wedlock. She expressed her new ideas in frank letters to her family in Zamora, no doubt smiling to imagine the shocked reactions of her half sisters. Yet in six years she would have to return to these people among whom were those who now thought of her as a renegade revolutionary and a lost soul. And not only return, but depend on them to rescue her from death.

In a photo dating from that year and obviously taken to send to her relatives, Amparo wears a cloche hat of contrasting colors with stylish flaps loose about her ears. She looks like a Spanish Amelia Earhart with a sculpted mouth and dimpled upper lip. Her large eyes stare out in a beguiling manner.

What an adventure her life became! Every weekday morning she walked from a nearby pensión to her new job in Madrid's first skyscraper *La Telefónica* on the Gran Vía. Its Art Deco elegance underscored her own entrance into the modern world. Whenever she passed through its monolithic lobby and swept her gaze upwards to the artwork on its vaulted ceilings, she must have exulted anew in her escape from her backwater beginnings.

By some miracle *La Telefónica* would survive the siege of Madrid. The fascist artillery used it as a bull's-eye, and it became famous for the number of direct hits it withstood. Arturo Barea in *The Forging of A Rebel* told what it was like to work and sleep while waiting for the shell that would do more than shatter the walls, more than kill the friend on the floor above.

In the evenings, Amparo strolled through the narrow streets off the *Gran Vía* searching for an available apartment. The neighborhood consisted mostly of older buildings with small bars and shops on their lower floors. One day she spotted a 'FOR RENT' sign on an ornate redbrick structure just two blocks behind her workplace. Zigzag arabesques and scrollwork decorated the walls and windows. Both the open balconies and the shuttered Moorish *miradors* were

adorned with curlicued ironwork. Number 17 Calle del Barco—
"Street of the Boat"—a charming name!

When she rang the *portera's* bell, a fragile young woman with a
limp answered. "May I see the apartment?" she asked.

"Of course! But it's very small." The woman's name was María
Cortes. She would become Amparo's good friend.

Amparo fell in love with the tiny two-room flat under the eaves.
She immediately hurried over to the owner's address and signed a
lease.

María Cortes remembered Amparo well. "She was the best of
women. She had such deep feelings, especially for poor people. I had
a very delicate back—they had operated on me when I was very
little—and would go upstairs to sunbathe on the roof because heat
relieved the discomfort. The moment Amparo heard my footsteps,
she would accompany me. We shared an enormous mutual liking
for one another. She was very Catholic, and often we went to Mass
together."

In her spare hours, Amparo treated herself to the movies on the
Gran Vía as well as concerts and readings at the *Ateneo*. There
she made friends with many musicians and artists. One night she
heard the young novelist Ramón J. Sender reading parts of his just-
published novel *Imán*. But she was too shy to push forward and
make his acquaintance.

Amparo also attended the literary gatherings at the cafés, including the group surrounding Valle-Inclán, the legendary Galician novelist. She happened to be there when he praised Ramón J. Sender's
Imán as the best novel of the new epoch. Papá, seated in back, complained modestly how, after signing the book contract, he had tried
to withdraw the novel because he was dissatisfied with it. He even
had returned the advance, but the publisher stuck to his legal rights
and printed the book.

They spoke that night for the first time. He remembered her face
from the *Ateneo* and later, when she stood up to leave, offered to
accompany her. They walked up San Jerónimo towards the Puerta
del Sol. Papá spoke about Valle-Inclán, a writer whose simple, modest nature he admired enormously.

Over coffee in her bohemian garret, he told her how as a four-
teen-year-old he had been suspended from school in Zaragoza and
began to live away from the family. He worked in a number of phar-

macies, continuing his studies, until at the age of eighteen he travelled to Madrid to escape his father. At the university he enrolled as a law student. When the famous flu epidemic closed the campus, he spent his days in the *Ateneo*'s library reading down one shelf and the next, sleeping on a bench in *Retiro* park and washing in the fountain called *La Joya*.

To pay for his meals, he wrote articles under a pseudonym. Also he involved himself in the student protests, and was arrested when the police found him nailing up anti-monarchist posters in the park. His father saved him from jail by claiming him as a minor and bringing him back to Huesca. The old man had just assumed the management of a small rural newspaper, *La Tierra*. Papá took over as the unofficial editor. When he turned twenty-one, he resumed classes at the University of Madrid. One year later he was drafted into the army. He served in the grossly mismanaged Moroccan campaign, and was discharged a second lieutenant. Out of these experiences he wrote *Imán* while working as a journalist for *El Sol*, the republican daily. Once this novel was published and his reputation established, he earned his living writing on his own. His articles and essays voiced the ideologies of the Spanish anarchists: the workers and peasants only had to free themselves from the Church and the ruling class for their innate idealism to blossom into a classless society of love and comradeship.

My aunt Conchita's daughter Ana María described a prank my father played during her childhood: "Once he came to our house when I was on a walk. When we returned, we found he had taken all my dolls and arranged them everywhere with such charm that they seemed alive! One was peeking through the curtains, others looking out the doors. Some were climbing the heating pipes, another hiding below the wardrobe! It frightened me because it seemed as if my dolls only waited until I was gone to come alive! I said, 'Mamá, why are all my dolls waiting for me?'"

Conchita took up the story. "Oh, if you only knew what my brother was like in those days! Look, I'm going to tell you an episode that occurred some years before he met Amparo. My husband Emi and I had to break off Pepe's engagement to Mercedinas, whose father was Commander-in-Chief of all the Spanish cavalry and an old friend of my father Don José. He lived in a palace in the Tetuan sector of Madrid and it had enormous gardens. Ah, this is a story! I was angry with Pepe a long time.

"Mercedinas was a great friend of Pepe's sister Maruja. I treated her like a little sister, but then Pepe started courting her.

"One day I said to him, 'Listen, don't play around with Mercedinas, eh? She's like one of the family.'

"And he replied, 'No, she's like a sister to me.' He was already twenty-five or six years old, and the girl eighteen.

Conchita changed voices with her characters. Pepe she portrayed self-important and wide-eyed.

"And I said, 'Good! But hold back a bit.' Because I had heard the girl was infatuated with him. One day I said to her, 'Listen, Mercedinas, what's going on with Pepe?'

Conchita projected Mercedinas in a petulant whisper. "'Look, I want to tell you, I want to say, Pepe and I are engaged. We're going to get married!'

"And I thought, how is this girl, with her father the Commander-in-Chief of the cavalry, going to marry Pepe? This man won't marry in a church! Would to God that he would! I would have liked that marriage because the girl was like a part of our family, incredibly beautiful, with four or five years of education at *Sacre Coeur* and a great deal of money. But he kept saying to me, 'Don't worry yourself, woman! I know what I'm doing.'

"'But the girl doesn't,' I told him. 'She's infatuated with you!'

"So he didn't change his behavior." Conchita picked up her fan. "Then one fine day Maruja said to me, rolling her eyes, 'Do you know that Pepe and Mercedinas are engaged, although they say they aren't?'

"I replied, 'I'm horrified! There's going to be a big quarrel between the families and it will be all his fault!'

"And Maruja, who was as big an idiot as Mercedinas, said, 'No, because if Mercedinas' family wants them to, they'll get married in the Church.'

She sat bolt upright. "'Can you see your brother dressed ceremonially, with a veiled bride at St. Joseph's and all the generals of Madrid seated in the pews? Don't be stupid!'

"A few days passed and then Mercedinas said to me, 'Conchita, you shouldn't call this stupid without knowing anything about it.'

"'*Andaaa!*'" Conchita tootled the incredulous expletive on two posthorn pitches. "'Look, Mercedinas, watch what you are doing. Pepe is my brother and has many good qualities, but I can't see you married to him.'

"'Yes, oh yes I will! And you know how Pepe says he won't go to Mass? Well, he says he'll give me whatever I want, so he'll go to Mass for me! So there!'

"'But he won't go to Mass! The day you marry, he'll stay home!'

"'Off with you!' she yelled. 'It's our business what we do!'

Conchita's fan increased in velocity. "Well, some days passed. We were busy planning for summer vacation. Maruja from one side and Mercedinas from the other still insisted Pepe would marry her. When we returned on the first of September, Pepe came to my house and said, 'Listen, Conchita, I must ask you and Emi a favor. You must ask for the hand of Mercedinas.'

"I was astonished! 'We have to ask for her hand and not Papá?'

"He avoided my eyes and stuttered excuses. 'Papá would have to come all the way from Zaragoza and it's a long trip and Papá's getting old, Papá—'

"I said, 'No, Papá travels! He always comes here on business. He's an intimate friend of the girl's grandfather. He would do it with pleasure!'

"'No, no, no, I don't want to bother Papá, no, no,'' Pepe replied. 'If you two do it, that's adequate.'

"Later, my husband Emi laughed when he heard about it. 'It's like a Hollywood movie!'

"'You might see it like that,' I said. 'But I'm disgusted!'

She slapped her thigh. "Well, we did it! The father gave Mercedinas a banquet in the garden on her saint's day, with everything beautifully arranged. Pepe had seated me with her and we had brought her a nice present. So we asked for her hand, and then I said to the father, 'Don Bonifacio, excuse us for having to leave early but my boy has very bad tonsilitis.'

"He called his official car with his chauffeur. And Pepe said, 'I'll go with you too.' He turned to Mercedinas. 'Look, I'll come back around eight and we'll go to the movies.'

The car had barely left the palace when Pepe said, 'But I can't marry this girl! I like her very much but I can't!'

"'Wicked!' I yelled. 'You made us ask for her hand! How could you do this to us? Now I understand why you didn't want Papá to come. We can get through this, but if Don José had come he would have killed you! Alive or dead, you would have married Mercedinas!''

My father once told a story about how he spent his evenings at this time among the striking workers, exchanging shots with the police. He was also taking Mercedinas to the movies in the afternoons. Mercedinas would send a note via an intermediary to ask what movie they were attending. Then the police were alerted not to arrest them because it would have caused a scandal for the family.

When he first met Amparo, my father was romantically involved with the daughter of the editor of *El Sol*. Amparo had heard tales of his predilection for affairs, but the anarchist ideal of Free Love also influenced her own awakening awareness. In October 1930, he began publishing a column in the CNT (*Confederación Nacional de Trabajo*) union's daily *Solidarid Obrera*, aligning himself with the unionists and mocking the Socialists who wished to govern without dissolving the monarchy. A planned rebellion fizzled that December, and the two officers shot, Galan and Hernandez, became working-class heroes. Student demonstrations erupted at the university. Then the April elections swept everyone away in rejoicing. The Second Republic was proclaimed, the royal family went into exile, and the citizenry danced in the streets for days. Not a policeman was to be seen, and yet not a single untoward incident occurred. Everyone wore red scarves and Phrygian caps. They carried flags, posters, even tree branches, and sang "The Marseillaise."

But the euphoria soon passed. Some monarchists met in the central area and played The Royal March on a phonograph. This infuriated the Sunday crowds who burned some cars. They marched to the offices of the monarchist newspaper, *ABC*, and set the building aflame. Martial law was proclaimed and the first innocent days of 'the new dawn' were over.

In July 1931 the telephone workers struck. The women were tired of low wages and poor treatment at the hands of the multinational monopoly. The government called out the civil guard and there were some shootings. The telephone workers felt betrayed because the Socialist leaders, who had promised their support, panicked. There was bad blood between the Socialist UGT (*Unión General de Trabajadores*) which more or less controlled Madrid and the telephone workers who belonged to the CNT. The UGT provided scabs and in their newspaper *El Socialista* attacked the CNT as anarchist provocateurs.

Amparo wrote a childhood friend at this time that she felt very persecuted. Living as she did just a few blocks from *La Telefónica*, she must have encountered many violent incidents on her street.

During the early days of the walkout, Pepe spotted her at the CNT offices where she had volunteered as a typist. He invited her to a meal and asked how she was supporting herself during the strike.

"I am teaching piano students at home," she said, not wanting him to know she was in financial straits.

"Why not take a job typing for me?" he asked. "I need a secretary. If I had known what a good typist you were, I would have asked you before."

'Secretary' was often a jokester's euphemism for something else, so she refused. "To help you with your manuscripts is one thing," she said. "But I'm determined to stay with the phone company."

They began to meet in the Plaza Santa Barbara at the outdoor café just across the street from the Pensión Bilbaina where Pepe lived. Amparo would bring freshly typed chapters of *Orden Publico*, his new book, and pick up his rough drafts. His radical friends frequently joined them and many intense political discussions took place. Pepe was heavily involved in the clandestine activities of the CNT which he felt was responding to the will of the people. His job was to relay coded phone instructions to other cities. Although Amparo never was a political activist, the events of the strike swept her up and she tried to enter the men's conversations. Often she left these meetings irritated by their condescending comments.

Not until two co-workers were wounded by assault guards did she become so enraged that she volunteered at union headquarters for a dangerous task. They needed someone to place a bomb on the floor that held the telephone switching equipment. She was given a small package and instructions. That evening at the appointed hour, she joined the crowd of protesters at La Telefónica, wearing her blue cloak to conceal what she carried. A scuffle was started at the front entrance to divert the guards. When events were at their most chaotic, she slipped in the side door. She avoided the elevators and ran upstairs. Once she had concealed the package, she returned.

The crowd cried, 'Scab, scab!' when she appeared, also a part of the plan. Her heart beating wildly, she ran in the direction of the Plaza Santa Barbara café where she found Pepe and a few others.

"Well, you are a bundle of nerves this evening," Pepe said.

Just then a distant explosion was heard and she jumped. "I did it!" she cried. "I placed the bomb!"

My father wrote about the incident in his novel *Seven Red Sundays*. His acquaintance, whom he called 'Graco,' looked at Amparo in astonishment.

"You?" he asked.

"Who else?" she said proudly. "Certainly me. Thousands of lines must be out of action."

Graco made a big fuss over her, kissing her hand and asking her how long she had been a member of the strike organization.

"Three months," Amparo replied, getting up and arranging her cloak.

"Where are you going now?" Pepe asked.

"Home to my tiny apartment," she said. "I must get some sleep because tomorrow I rise early to confess and go to Mass."

"To confess?" The men's mouths gaped in astonishment.

"Yes, about the bomb. But I won't tell the priest when or where it was. If he absolves me, well and good. If not, all the worse for him. My conscience is clear."

Pepe burst out laughing, but Graco was enraged. However they did not taunt Amparo as a petite bourgeoise any more. The bomb did considerable damage but no one was hurt. Pepe and Amparo's relationship continued upon the firm base of their collaboration.

"I treated Amparo like a sister from the first time we met," Conchita declared. "Pepe was sick in bed with a flu at the Pensión Bilbaina and I went to visit him. Amparo arrived to deliver a typed manuscript and he introduced her to me as his secretary. Some time later, Emi and I went to the movies on the *Gran Vía*, to the Galería. And I said, 'Well, look who bought good seats!' They had those white armchairs in the mezzanine at the time. And Emi said, 'It's Pepe with someone! Where'd you meet her, Pepe?'

"'She's my secretary,' Pepe said and frowned at us. 'I don't remember where I met her.'

"'You're acting just like an American,' Emi said. 'Obviously this is the secretary you've been searching for.'

"And Pepe said, 'No I haven't been looking especially. This just happened. She's been working at the telephone company.'

"'I'm going to give classes in piano until the strike's settled,' Amparo said. 'Ramón asked me to be his secretary and I said, "Oh, no!"'

"When Emi and I were ready to leave after the movie, we went back to them, and I said, 'Let's go for coffee.' They didn't even know we were there until Pepe looked up and said, 'No-no-no! We're staying until everyone leaves!'

"When they left hand-in-hand, we were still standing at the curb. A street urchin looked up from his shoeshine kit and said, 'Hey, just look at those two lovebirds!' She captured a boy's teasing tone. 'I think there's going to be a wedding!'

"'No, no, no!' they said.

"Later my husband said, 'This time he'll marry for sure! Even before we get to know her because she's extremely beautiful and tall.'"

Conchita's fan started up again. "So that was the winter of 1931. If my brother had said they must go to Hell, Amparo would have gone with him. That's the way she was. That summer in San Rafael, Emi and I met a pretty woman, one of those delicate Andalusian types from Murcia, brunette and well brought up. Friends thought of introducing her to Pepe but I said, 'No, no, Pepe already has a love, this secretary of his, and this time he'll marry!' She smiled at the memory. "And by the winter of '32, although they would not admit it, they were engaged."

A sonnet my father wrote in later years described Amparo as he remembered her from this time. Although she is not mentioned by name, the context makes the subject of the poem obvious:

> Instead of the truth came you,
> my bride of strikes and unions,
> all aflutter with your enthusiasms
> and a red star on each shoe.
> You saw me in your competition,
> her promiscuity and my innate qualities,
> doubting between Yahweh and Beelzebub,
> you came to give me your contradictions.
> I knew no more of the world, beloved,
> bristling with spines like a ripe cactus,
> than what you told me in your ecstasy.
> Yet in that hypocrisy of your silence
> I behold myself as on the premature
> anniversary of my death you saw me.

The telephone strike failed and Amparo was out of a job. She wrote letters to several ministries asking for employment and searched for more piano students.

In September, Pepe left for Paris and Berlin to attend writers' congresses and meet with foreign publishers. He returned pessimistic about conditions in Europe, especially Germany where the depression was playing into the hands of the Nazis. In Spain many violent incidents occurred between the civil guards and the peasants whose situation was desperate. But the general feeling was that the wrongs of centuries could not be corrected overnight. Amparo, meanwhile, concentrated on her music. That winter she played some recitals with her violinist friend Antonio Arias and practiced for a concert of Spanish composers.

In January 1933, just after Hitler was elected chancellor in Germany, the Casas Viejas massacre occurred in which assault guards brutally murdered a peasant family. My father immediately left to cover the incident and was the first journalist to arrive. His eyewitness reports, gathered at considerable personal risk, were published in *La Libertad*. The government tried to suppress them and put out an order for his arrest. One day Amparo heard a knock on her door.

"Quick, hide me somewhere!" Pepe said, breathless from running. "The police are after me! Azaña is outraged by what I've written. They spotted me outside my pensión!"

The police came to the concierge María Cortes and asked her, "Do you know a certain Ramón J. Sender?"

"Well, no," she replied. "I can tell you nothing. The name doesn't ring a bell."

After they left, she ran upstairs and said, "Señorita Amparo, listen, Don Ramón shouldn't show his face! Don't let him go outside because the police are looking for him."

He stayed with Amparo several days until things calmed down, and during this time their relationship became intimate. Azaña later admitted that Sender's reports contributed considerably to the defeat of his government. When parliament decided to investigate the Casas Viejas affair, the police search ended and he was free to roam the city again. But by then he was more or less living with Amparo. Together they attended the May Day celebrations. Not a single car moved in the city, not even a trolley.

María Cortes, the concierge, reported: "One day, in the middle of Mass, Amparo turned to me and said, 'I have to go, María.' And she left. When I returned to the house, I asked, 'Why did you leave, Señorita Amparo?'

"She said, 'Look, I couldn't stay. I believe in God, but since Ramón has been with me, I am totally devoted to him. If I cannot visit the house of God with devotion, I prefer not to go.'

"From then on, Amparo never returned to church. At the beginning, Amparo didn't want me to know she was living with your father. But I said, 'Look, Señorita Amparo, these conventions are silly. Your fiancé can stay here.' So that's the way it was."

Late in May, my father left on a five-month journey to Russia as a guest of the *Unión Internacional de Escritores*. He returned generally sympathetic with the Soviet cause, although his published views avoided a blind acceptance of Marxist-Stalinist ideologies. He praised the egalitarianism he observed, and was especially impressed by a message the writers' organization received asking for help shovelling snow in the streets. He felt it necessary to justify his intellectual career to the workers: "I write books and articles because I don't know how to mix concrete, tan leather or conduct a tram . . ." Although other visiting Spaniards criticized the lack of civil liberties, my father accepted the explanation that it expressed the spontaneous self-discipline of the masses. For the next three years he would align himself increasingly with the Communists until his final disillusionment during the Spanish Civil War.

In *Seven Red Sundays*, one of the main characters, Samar, writes a love letter to his woman friend Amparo, an expression of love which my father could well have sent my mother at this time.

Dearest, forgive me:
Until now, seven o'clock, I couldn't write you. I'm not going to write much, but you know I love you, little darling, desperately. I am hungry for your arms and your lips. I would like to give you a life filled with light and peace. But I don't believe it can be . . . I want for you all the peace and quietness that shines in my soul when I lose myself in our love. But how can I give you the peace and quietness that are so far away from me? . . . I have known life in its most secret corners, in sweetness and in bitterness. I believed my soul held all the secrets, knew everything, had reached everything . . . Suddenly, I came to know you . . . I was drunk every day with the light in my own heart . . . I found in the depths of your gentle eyes the secret of the universe, immense and everlasting, and my heart quickened in beats of joy . . . You and me, darling! You and me! Others don't exist.

In the general election in Spain that November, the Right gained more seats than the squabbling Socialists. Street fights occurred between militant student groups. Many people remained unemployed. But these alarming events swirled harmlessly around Papá and Amparo, snug in their love nest. They tended to stay home in spite of friends' complaints about their "overextended honeymoon" and their "annoyingly bourgeois" attitudes. But the criticisms bounced off them harmlessly.

"The natural egoism of lovers is threatening to others, because they see the materialism of their own lives condemned," Papá commented.

María Cortes: "Your parents stayed until she became pregnant with you. One day she said, 'María, we're going to move to Monteleón Street. We've found an apartment there because this one is so small.'"

My father told Conchita he was leaving his pensión and moving to an apartment.

"You're taking an apartment by yourself?" She shook her head in dismay. "What dirty sheets and socks you'll have! Who will buy you a necktie when yours falls away in tatters?"

"No!" he replied with a laugh. "I won't be by myself."

"So then with whom?"

"You're a witch, you're supposed to know everything! I won't tell you with whom."

"All right, it's Amparo," Conchita said.

"So it doesn't matter if I bring her over to visit?"

"Of course it doesn't matter, neither to Emi or me. She's a young woman who's acting stupidly because she loves you very much. And we'll come to your house also and toast your health! For me, it's as if you are married! Right now! If you tell me later that it was just a passing affair, I won't listen! I won't tolerate it. Don't come by in a couple of months whining, 'Oh look, I don't like her! Now I'm with another.'"

These were the so-called "Black Years," the right-wing Radicals in power cynically undoing the few reforms of Azaña's cabinet and selling government favors to their cronies. Spain was overwhelmed with literature on Russia. My father produced two books from his summer journey, *Madrid-Moscú* and *Carta de Moscú sobre el Amor*. In the latter he attacked the repressive sexual mores of the Catholic Church as the cause of alienation and superstition. The erotic symbolism of religion was utilized by old maids and failed lovers for their own titillation. In contrast, he exalted Soviet sex as free from mysticism, 'open' marriage as the means to achieving true tranquillity and fidelity in the home. Where sexual liberty was absolute, there existed much less libertinism than within the religiously repressive systems.

Amparo labored long hours at the typewriter that winter. As a result my father published a total of five books in 1934, mostly derived from his articles. By the time the manuscripts went to the printer, Amparo knew she was pregnant. Conchita was carrying her third child and they spent much time together.

Papá placed his most radical articles in *La Lucha*, the daily which for a year replaced the banned *Solidaridad Obrera*. It promoted the concept of a single front to unite all leftist parties against the counterrevolution and was frequently confiscated by the police. On several occasions he had to go into hiding after an issue hit the stands.

There was constant turmoil in the streets. That spring, the Rightist leader Robles held a Nazi-style rally at the Escorial, and Madrid's workers expected a Mussolini-like march on the capital. But bad weather kept the crowd below the predicted number.

In retrospect, those early years were to seem idyllic because that October, three events electrified Spain: a general strike, the government of Catalonia's proclamation of an autonomous state and, most serious of all, an armed rebellion by the miners in Asturias.

MUTUALIDAD
DEL
CLERO ESPAÑOL

Reintégrese

A. № 711957

CERTIFICACION DE PARTIDA DE BAUTISMO

Parroquia *de San Juan Bautista*
Población *ZAMORA*
Diócesis *Zamora*
Provincia *Zamora*
Libro *1896 - 1924*
Folio *128*
Núm. *500*

Notas marginales
Se confirmó en esta parroquia el 8 de julio el 1922 - M. Barrido - Rubricado. -

Don *Casimiro Sastre Sastre*,
Encargado del Archivo *de San Juan Bautista de Zamora*
Diócesis de *Zamora*,
CERTIFICA: Que según consta del acta reseñada al margen, correspondiente al Libro de Bautismos,
D.ª *María del Amparo Barayón Miguel*,
fué BAUTIZADO el día *22* de *mayo* de *1904*,
Nació el día *8* de *mayo* de *1904*,
en la calle ___, n.º ___,
siendo natural de ___, Diócesis de ___
Provincia de ___
PADRES: D. *Antonio Barayón*
natural de *Feleas de Arriba (Zamora)*
y de D.ª *Isabel Miguel*
natural de *El Perdigón (Zamora)*
ABUELOS PATERNOS, D. *José Barayón*
natural de *Villaperdós*
y D.ª *Casimira Ascona*
natural de *Aguilar*
ABUELOS MATERNOS, D. *Quintín Miguel*
natural de *El Perdigón*
y D.ª *Eugenia Vaquero*
natural de *El Perdigón*
PADRINOS: D. *Saturnino Barayón y D.ª Maximina Miguel*
MINISTRO: *D. José Campos*
Zamora a *10* de *junio* de *1988*

(Firma del Encargado del Archivo)
(Sello)

(Para otras Diócesis)
Obispado de ___
V.º B.º,
El Vicario General,

Modelo exclusivo de la Mutualidad del Clero Español, para la expedición en los Archivos Eclesiásticos.
PRECIO DE ESTE IMPRESO, DIEZ PESETAS

Amparo's baptism certificate, an important document because it fixed her birth date. Also it lists her Aunt Maximina (who later was to take over my care when Amparo was arrested) as her godmother.

Antonio Barayón with his children. Back row, left to right: *Casimira, Saturnino, Magdalena, and Amparo.* Front row: *Antonio, Nati, and Eugenia. Circa 1913.*

The Barayón family's Café Iberia as it looked during Amparo's childhood. Note the piano on the balcony.

*Amparo with her niece Magdalena Maes and two neigh-
borhood boys. Circa 1928. Amparo was twenty-four years
old.*

Amparo Barayón at twenty-six, recently arrived in Madrid.

A photograph of Amparo dated June 21, 1929, and inscribed "to my goddaughter with love, Amparito." She was twenty-five years old. Courtesy of Antonio Arias.

*The Sender homestead in Chalamera, Aragon, where Ra-
món J. Sender was born.*

Ramón J. Sender circa 1922. He is approximately twenty-one.

Amparo Barayón with newborn Monchín (the author), November 1934 in Madrid. Photograph the author received from his Aunt Maruja in Mexico City, 1973.

Grandmother Andrea Garcés de Sender. This photo was found in Ramón J. Sender's wallet after his death.

Grandfather José Sender.

CHAPTER 6

RED OCTOBER TO
JULY 1936

I N response to the miners' revolt, the government brought in the Foreign Legion and Moorish mercenaries under the command of General Franco. Press censorship kept the people from learning the more gruesome details immediately, but rumors of the Moors' cruelty and the sexual tortures used by the civil guard horrified everyone. By the end of the month, thirty thousand leftists comprised of Republicans and Socialists were in prison. Most of their leaders were either dead, in jail or in hiding.

My father journeyed north to cover the Foreign Legion's recapture of Oviedo at a cost of three thousand dead, seven thousand wounded. He was outraged by the atrocities perpetrated by the Moors against women and children. When he returned home, Madrid was still under martial law. Three days earlier, Amparo had gone into labor. She left a note at the apartment and went to the clinic. There the nuns seemed more preoccupied with the dreaded revolution than with her labor pains. She gave birth to a son at two in the morning to the accompaniment of machine-gun fire in the street.

Two days later, Papá arrived at her bedside. He had walked to the clinic with his hands raised above his head to prove to the patrols he was unarmed. He stared in amazement at the scrawny little bundle in her arms. My head was misshapen from the passage through the birth canal, my skin purple and eyelids swollen.

"He's very intelligent," he muttered, trying to hide his growing panic. "It can be seen in the shape of his head."

Amparo laughed at his expression. "He is just fine, *querido*, although a little underweight. And his head will not remain pointed for long."

According to Conchita, Papá was an exaggerated father, worrying about the slightest thing. My birth created a new problem for my parents because family pressure on them to get married increased, especially from my grandfather Don José. Papá and his father, both strong personalities, had a terrible relationship. As the eldest son, Papá had borne the brunt of Don José's temper throughout his childhood, and his ongoing defiance remained a source of much family friction. Yet ultimately Amparo would be the one to pay with her life for their flouting of traditional values.

Conchita: "What your parents did not want, either of them—this, well, really it doesn't matter but—" She drew a big breath. "They didn't want to get married! I remember once saying to your father, 'Look, when one has to go somewhere, Pepe, it's better to take the highway and not strike out cross-country. Why make your children's lives more difficult? You two have the right to live however you want and to me it's the same, but the children!' But they always said to me, 'We're happy the way we are!'"

She remembered Papá bringing Amparo home from the clinic. It was a brilliant autumn day. After the antiseptic smells of the clinic, Amparo inhaled the fall fragrances with delight. There had been a lull in the street fighting. Crowds strolled along the boulevards in the warm sunshine, as if both violent death and laughter were natural ingredients in the life of a Spaniard. They turned up Calle del Divino Pastor, a street of little shops that connected with theirs. Papá held me with a new father's awkwardness. A pockfaced junkman, remarkable for the long wisps of hair extending from his ears, lifted his cap from beside his cart.

"Welcome home, *señora*," he said. And to Papá he said, 'You are Sender, right? You write for *La Lucha* these days."

On the steps of their apartment house, children were playing with spent bullet casings they had collected in the street. They clustered around us saying what people always say. "What's his name? What's his name?"

Amparo smiled. "Ramón, of course, like his father. Little Monchín."

"Monchín, Monchín!" they cried.

Conchita visited one day to find Amparo changing me. Obviously I had not emptied my bladder because I let go a fountain across her dress. Amparo was embarrassed, but Conchita was used to it from her own babies. She kept staring at me because I was a perfect miniature Don José—just like my grandfather.

"Please, don't mention the resemblance to Ramón," Amparo begged. "It will cause trouble."

That winter all of Spain remained polarized, but the Left did not interpret the outcome of the Red October events as a failure. At least it had proved the working class would not tolerate the establishment of a fascist state. However it had been a defeat for the socialist cause, and the trial of the imprisoned leaders continued throughout that winter.

For Amparo and Papá, these disturbances were peripheral. He stayed home to write his new novel *Mr. Witt among the Rebels*, a fictionalized description of the First Republic's struggles in 1873 to resolve issues similar to those in the 1930s. When I was restless, Amparo lulled me with Chopin waltzes on the piano. She overlaid the harmonies with all her heart's fulfillment, coaxing a beautiful tone from her old upright.

Papá questioned everyone about childcare. "What's that?" he asked. "Why are you doing that? Tell me everything about babies."

He and Amparo bothered their pediatrician so much that when they phoned him he would say, 'What, more nonsense? What's the matter this time?'

In the spring, they took happy rambles, with me in a borrowed perambulator. At the zoo, Papá introduced me to the elephants and hippopotamus for the first time, holding me up to blink over the railing. I did not seem impressed.

"To him everything is extraordinary," Papá explained. "He sees no difference between God and the camel."

Marcelle, my French aunt who later would lose her husband, my father's favorite brother Manolo, to the falangist execution squad, recalled meeting Amparo at this time. "I met her when Manolo and I returned from our honeymoon in February. She was much taller than your father's sisters. When she was dressed to go out, she was very attractive. One day I went with friends to meet her at the theater. We were in the balcony and Amparo was seated below. She was wearing a lovely hat—it was the beginning of spring—a circlet of violets. At the intermission, Amparo and her hat came out to join us.

"Amparo had much character and willpower. She certainly wasn't a coquette like the Sender sisters. Not Amparo. She was a little austere, a woman of intellect above all, more intellectual than the sisters of her husband, more reserved. She became perturbed if other women flirted with your father. Amparo did not confide her fears to me, but obviously Pepe enjoyed the company of other women. He was not the sort who should have married, because he preferred the bachelor's life."

What a happy time for Amparo! Papá hardly went out, her baby was healthy and her milk abundant. In her music, she had an avenue of expression, and her typing was an invaluable help to her lover. But the political crisis continued, although martial law was downgraded to a "state of alarm" renewed from month to month. The rightists took their cues from the European dictatorships and proposed "a national revolution against atheism and the international threat of the Marxists, Masons and Jews." The leftists saw themselves on the road towards a Russian-style purge of the ruling class.

The reactionary government of Lerroux favored the rich and returned the Jesuits' confiscated properties. They appointed General Franco chief of staff and shelved land reform as well as public education projects. When the hot summer days came, Amparo took the train with me, Conchita and her children to Villa Frutos where Papá would join us on the weekend.

Conchita: "How we loved that first breath of the Sierras after the heat of Madrid, the smell of sage from the rocky hillsides. Our stop, San Rafael, was the first on the other side of the peak of *Alto de León*. Emi and I had rented the downstairs and Pepe and Amparo the second floor. We had our new baby Riqui, only a few months younger than you."

When my father arrived with some friends, we picnicked in the pines. I was told I met my first cows there, and looked at them with the same expression I had given the zoo animals, as if thinking, "more strange creatures."

"Yes, you are right," Papá said to me. "They are all as strange as you think they are. And just like us, they did not ask to be born."

He looked over his shoulder at Amparo. "We are all innocents, here on this planet without reason or motive."

"But do you believe in God?' Amparo asked him.

"Sometimes, but sometimes not. I see God in the nature of men. Sometimes I believe in men and sometimes not." He grinned. "All without reason."

His paradoxes always annoyed Amparo. "Ramón, why don't you answer me seriously?" she complained.

"I'm as serious as possible in the presence of a kissable angel," he replied.

He thought Amparo a marvelous innocent. Yet if he told her, she would lose the very quality he held so precious. At the same time, Amparo felt he didn't respect her ideas enough. After all, she was a serious person with ideas of her own which she enjoyed discussing. She considered his attitude patronizing and often told him so in a flare of temper. He found her incomprehensible and enchanting.

That day, one of the men had a pistol. They took turns shooting at a distant rock. The women found it nerve-wracking but the children were fascinated. Suddenly smoke began to drift from the nearby bushes. The crackle of twigs brought everyone to their feet.

"Fire!" Ramón yelled.

He grabbed his leather jacket and began beating at the flames. They labored to contain the blaze, but it had been a rainless summer and the brush was like tinder. The best they could do was escape before they were caught by the foresters and accused of arson.

"A bullet must have struck a spark," someone said.

The fire burned out of control for hours in spite of the arrival of the fire department. The men watched the smoke from the chalet with the guilty expression of boys who knew they had done something wrong. Politics had been banned at the dinner table for the duration of vacation, so instead Papá told a silly story of his youth (which I recall his telling me years later).

"Once I borrowed an old nag to ride to the swimming hole," he said. "We used to swim there naked. After a while, getting cold, I decided to ride my somewhat crazy horse a short distance into the sunshine to dry off. Her broad back was a pleasant place to sunbathe. Anyway, I was stretched out, my eyes closed, when she took off down the main road. I barely managed to stay on, and no matter how hard I pulled at the reins, she refused to stop. It was suppertime by her reckoning and she had the bit in her teeth. We came into the middle of town at a canter and completely broke up a procession of the Daughters of Mary. They all screamed and beat at me with various objects while the mayor and the bishop talked about the scandals of liberalism."

"No politics!" Amparo warned amidst general laughter.

I participated in the children's games mainly by interfering. When a wrestling match between two boys bowled me into a corner, I wailed piteously.

Papá squatted down and hit his own head against the wall. "Ow!" he cried, making a clownish grimace and rolling his eyes. By the third repetition, my tears stopped. I crawled to the wall and butted it, sitting back and glancing up for approval. Papá grinned. "See, little son, a man laughs at pain," he said. "He must be courageous in this best and worst of all possible worlds." Gradually, I learned I was something different from Amparo. I must find my fulfillment in the world of men, and be strong and independent. 'No' was the first word I said. I was a vigorous crawler and would disappear in an instant into the flower beds to eat dirt by the handful. Luckily the yard was below the level of the high road and Ana María old enough to bring me back if I wandered. At night, Amparo put me to sleep singing the lullaby for which Papá had written the words. She used a melody from one of the canticles of St. John of the Cross:

> "Four little ducks
> Who had a mama
> Played at skiprope
> Near the water
> Little red beaks
> Little white feathers
> They played and played
> Not paying attention to anything."

When Conchita sang it, the melody evoked an image of Amparo in a blue and white speckled sweater, her sleeves rolled back, bathing me in a tub on the kitchen floor. I dreamt this as a child and always treasured it as the one concrete memory I retained of her, her dark hair tied back, the sunlight sparkling off the water.

"In the second verse, a wolf creeps up on them," Conchita explained. She leaned back and smoothed out her skirt. "So that was how it was. The mountains, the forest glades, the profusion of wildlife all fed our spirits after months of city living. In the mornings, Pepe walked into the village for the newspapers. Every three or four days he would grow restless and take the train to Madrid to pick up his mail, phone a few friends or deliver an article. Because of the censorship, he could only write on innocuous subjects such as foreign writers or the theater. He always returned with bad news: the reimposition of martial law in Barcelona or Franco's staging army maneuvers in Asturias as a warning to the miners. Azaña, who had barely escaped with his life after the October Revolution, spent the summer in front of large audiences, calling for the Left to unite. Largo Caballero inflamed the socialist youth with revolutionary rhetoric while Prieto, from his exile in Paris, ignored leftist criticism and worked for unity with the Republicans."

"Just forget the world for a few months, Ramón," Amparo would beg. "It won't stop spinning."

He would agree. "Even though after a few days I can't bear the sight of another tree, another vacuous cow, I know I belong out here," he told her. "At heart I am a *baturro*, a hardheaded Aragonese rustic."

In September we returned to Madrid where an electrical calm prevailed. The airing of the Straperlo roulette machine bribery case implicated government officials and precipitated Prime Minister Lerroux's resignation. With the announcement that November of an even more lurid scandal involving Lerroux himself, the reactionary government found itself publicly disgraced and new elections were scheduled for February. The right-wing parties plastered the streets with posters but offered no platform, confident they would restore the power of the army, Church and ruling class. In contrast, a newly formed coalition of the Left named the Popular Front printed a manifesto which carefully outlined a program including amnesty for the Red October prisoners and the completion of the 1931 reforms. It took its name from the Popular Front campaign against fascism which the Communist International had approved the previous summer, an ill-fated choice because other nations were to interpret the Popular Front's victory as a Marxist takeover.

My father was finishing *Mr. Witt among the Rebels*, Amparo urging him to complete it in time to submit to the National Literature contest. She was always at the typewriter whenever he slept so she could make fresh copies of his scribbled-over drafts.

One evening Amparo phoned Conchita. "Ramón has bought a

revolver from a friend," she said. "He says we must prepare for the worst. I had wanted to tell him I was pregnant again, that we must find a larger place, but how—"

"Amparo, stay calm," Conchita told her. "Are you sure you're pregnant?"

"Yes, I'm already beginning to show," Amparo replied. "I think the baby will come in February."

"Now you must get married," Conchita insisted. "Otherwise you're only thinking of yourselves. Consider the children! Why place daggers under their feet?"

"You behave as if they were yours!"

"Well, it's as if they were mine!" Conchita told her. "I don't want my children entering life on a bad path. No sir!"

Conchita sat upright with a determined expression. "I must have finally convinced them, because one day Pepe said, 'Listen, the Republic has legalized civil ceremonies so we're going to get married at the Escorial and you have to come along.'

One morning that same month, Papá borrowed a car and drove everyone to the Escorial. The wedding was held in a small parish house, a retired judge presiding. Emi and Conchita were the sponsors and two employees of the judge were witnesses. Amparo wore a simple navy blue wool suit and little matching hat, Papá his usual worn garbardine.

Although Amparo notified her family, no one attended. However shortly afterwards, her younger brother Antonio came to visit. In a family photo, he wears an elegant suit and rimless glasses, giving the impression of an intellectual young scientist. Supposedly he was the only one in her family who could tolerate her way of life.

"My brother Antonio visited and we went out to supper," Amparo told Conchita. She mentioned how happy she was to see him, to have a member of her family near. He was somewhat shy around Pepe, but alone with her he told her his electrical business was prospering and the family was doing well.

The civil marriage displeased my grandfather Don José enormously. Conchita's sister Asunción reported, "For my father, marriage did not exist outside the Church. 'No, they aren't married!' he insisted, and continued addressing Amparo as 'señorita.' Of course it didn't matter to me. We often said, 'Look, Papá, you may call her want you like, but we're treating them as a married couple.'"

"There are minds in this world which are outside the usual order of things," Conchita said, speaking of my father. "You can't box them in. Never! I remember Pepe coming over to my apartment one morning in despair. Andrea had not yet been born, your mother having a few more months to go.

" 'I'm here!' he said.

" 'I see you,' I replied. 'Whom have you fought with now?'

"And he said with much drama, 'With whom do you think? With Amparo!'

"I said, 'I'm sorry for her. I'll phone her right away to calm her.'

" 'No!' he shouted. 'But since I haven't had a meal, I came here to eat.'

" 'Don't even dream of it,' I told him.

"And he said, 'Now I see that Amparo is more your sister than my wife!'

" 'Well, just about,' I replied. 'At least we're faithful and remain in agreement. Even if it's against you. Never come to this house without Amparo, either to snack or have a meal. Either the two of you come, or nobody comes.'

" 'I'm not eating at home!' he yelled.

" 'Eat where you want,' I told him, 'but here . . . you don't eat.' "
She had captured Papá's inflections perfectly, and her replies were cold Toledo steel. " 'I'm phoning Amparo to tell her, "Rest tranquil, let it be, because he certainly won't eat anywhere the way he is, acting so crazy. You feed your little boy and then go take a nap. After a while Pepe will show up. When he does, you should say to him, 'Don't you understand that you have met the woman whom God made for you?' " 'Because my brother could not understand this. He had a big heart, he was a good man, but—*carrammmba!*—to live with him—! And I told Amparo this when she was still single. Before she married him I said, 'Amparo, you are putting yourself in a situation that's going to bring you anguish. Think about it.' 'No, no, I've already thought about it,' she said to me. 'I've thought it through.' "

At the beginning of January 1936, my father was informed that his novel *Mr. Witt among the Rebels* had been awarded the National Prize. His picture appeared in all the papers. And on February 3, Papá's birthday, Amparo went into labor. Andrea was born at home four hours later, an easy delivery compared to the many hours it had taken me to arrive.

Two weeks later, the Popular Front won the elections and the celebrations and parades were endless. The prison gates were forced open by cheering crowds and all the prisoners were freed, both political and criminal alike. Many aristocrats fled the country and took exaggerated tales of communist atrocities with them. Elsewhere in Europe, fascism was on the march. Mussolini invaded Abyssinia and Hitler reoccupied the Rhineland.

Andrea's arrival, Conchita told me, caused me some difficulties. Although I was almost weaned, I was in the habit of returning to Amparo's breast now and then. Suddenly my place was usurped by this squalling bundle. Amparo made a special effort to reassure me. Also she found a fifteen-year-old niece of her old concierge María to be my nursemaid, a sweet-faced girl named Dionisia. I called her 'Aisia' and then everyone did. She adored my parents.

María: "One day your father came to me and said, 'Amparo is giving birth.' So I went over and there was the midwife and so on. We talked about my cousin Dionisia becoming your nursemaid. I said, 'Ah, what a pity that she's so young! Well, let's see if she can do the job.'

"Amparo said, 'It's not important how old she is. She just has to be nursemaid to Monchín.'

"'Well, if you want her, I'll bring her,' I said. So I brought Dionisia and she started working there.

Conchita: "I remember you walking beside Aisia, moving your elbow back and forth like a piston and shouting, 'By myself! By myself!'"

Marcelle: "You moved to the top floor of an apartment house on the Avenida Menendez Pelayo facing the lions' house in the Retiro zoo. When your father had worked all night long at the typewriter, your mother went out on the balcony where she kept a low table and typed there so as not to disturb her husband's rest. A very intelligent woman. And when she arose in the morning, she combed her dark hair with a few drops of water and pinned it behind her head with an aquamarine.

"She always helped her husband whom she loved and admired. She understood he was not like other men. He wrote when he felt like it, sometimes all night long. He made his own schedule, and she adjusted to it. Most women would have found him impossible, but she remained very devoted. To live with your father, a woman had to have all the virtues: good in bed, capable of running the household, of editing and typing his books. All these things Amparo did very well. What she lacked was the flirtatiousness Pepe found attractive. She would not put on airs or primp. But Pepe liked dressy women, and she did not do enough to satisfy him in this regard. Instead, she cultivated an interest in literature to retain an advantage over other women. And of course she had two children on her hands. She lived in the heaven of her husband."

The closeness of the animals excited me, the trumpeting of the elephants and the roars of the big cats. I would stand on the balcony to stare at the giraffes swaying like palm trees. And before falling asleep, I made Aisia tell me a story about the three little boats painted on my crib. But certain things frightened me, such as the peacocks' cries on the mornings I wet my bed. '*Me-yoon!*' they screamed. 'Bed-wetter!' And I was afraid of the civil guards in their dark capes in the park.

Sometimes Papá entertained mysterious men with unshaven cheeks. I looked them over carefully, ignoring their attempts to make friends. Then I would frown and give them their hats. Or tugging them to their feet, I pulled them towards the door. It was my way of telling them to leave.

"I played a game with you," Conchita told me. "I would say, 'Bring me a book of Paye's,'—that was your way of saying 'Papá.' You would go to the bookcase, take a book from the lowest shelf and bring it to me. All the books on that shelf were by Pepe, so you always succeeded at your task. But visitors unaware of this marvelled at how intelligent you were. Oh!" She laughed and slapped her knee. "I just remembered something! Don José came to meet your sister. He was very proud of his grandchildren, but Pepe was always ill at ease during these visits. He was especially irritated by Don José's insistence that both you children be baptized. Anyway, you must have sensed your father's mood because you decided to bring Grandpa his hat to encourage his departure.

"'No, no, not yet,' Pepe told you.

"You were disappointed and took the hat back to the hall. Suddenly you had to make pee-pee. Perhaps the hat reminded you of your potty, because you peed in Grandpa's hat, an event which made Pepe shout with laughter. You had expressed his feelings towards his father to perfection!

"However Don José managed to convince Amparo to baptize her children. Behind your father's back, they took you both to a local church for the brief ceremony."

The euphoria of the Popular Front victory soon gave way to rumors of a rightist coup. Groups of youths roamed the streets provoking incidents that could be blamed on the Reds. The government seemed incapable of stopping the political assassinations. When the hot summer days began, the adults all expected the worst but hoped against hope things would remain calm.

In *Counterattack in Spain*, my father recalled the mood of the days just before the Civil War began:

> At the beginning of July 1936, we were all in confusion and anxiety. Like everyone else, I expected the explosion. As it seemed that the military had not decided, and as the state of Madrid was enervating—victory, the hurry to organize it, the need of consolidating it, the joy of having routed everything in Spain that represented reaction, dirt, barbarism, and death—I, who didn't know how to begin to work in such an atmosphere, went to the country. I took a little house within less than a mile of San Rafael, a summer resort of the wealthy Madrid bourgeoisie among pine forests behind the mountainous mass of the Guadarrama.
>
> I had been there before. As I supposed that it would be a nest of vipers, I did not put the lease in my own name, and I gave my address to nobody so that letters would not come to me. Now and again I went to Madrid to collect my mail and reply to it. San Rafael is two hours' distance by train from the capital and actually is in the province of Segovia, whose boundary with Madrid runs along the high crests of the Guadarrama Range. I was far from imagining the importance to be taken by these lovely landscapes in the civil war and in the most intimate events of my life.

With Amparo's return to San Rafael, she moved one day's journey closer to Zamora and the unimaginable destiny awaiting her there. If only the Civil War had begun two weeks earlier or our vacation plans had been delayed, we would have remained safe in Madrid.

CHAPTER 7

SAN RAFAEL AND
EL ESPINAR

I N July 1982, forty-six years after my last journey with Amparo to San Rafael, I returned once again. I had been eagerly anticipating this search for Villa Frutos, the chalet which played such an important role at the beginning of my life and the war. Maruchi Rivera, one of the two daughters of the Director of Mountains whom Amparo took with her to Zamora in 1936, agreed to accompany me and my wife. Her response to my *El País* letter had helped fill in the story of those panic-stricken days.

It was a beautiful day. The Guadarrama foothills resemble the California Sierras with their golden fields and green swatches of forest. To the west I saw the huge cross that marked *El Valle De Los Caidos*, Franco's monument to the Civil War dead and his own final resting place. Thousands of loyalist prisoners had been condemned to years at hard labor carving the gigantic mausoleum out of solid rock. It was not on our itinerary. Franco only became commander in chief because all others who outranked him were killed. The most grotesque demise was General Sanjurjo's whom the Republic had sent into exile in Portugal after an abortive coup attempt. When the uprising began on July 18, a small plane was dispatched by rebellious officers to bring him back. He insisted on packing his dress uniform and medals in his suitcase. The added weight forced the plane into the trees at the end of the runway and Sanjurjo died in the crash. 'Vanity of vanities,' as Amparo's Sergeant Aguirre wrote to her.

The landscape coaxed my thoughts back to the present. We were driving along the *La Coruña* Highway, Spain's major northwest arterial. Papá and Maruchi's parents had crossed this countryside in a sixteen-hour trek, just minutes ahead of the artillery shells and bombs. The smell of sage from the mountain meadows evoked a familiar feeling instead of any visual recognition of the landscape.

Maruchi sang Amparo's lullaby, the same one Conchita had sung, but only the second verse about a mother wolf sneaking up to grab the baby in the bed. The imagery had darkened into a strange presentiment of what would occur. She gave the date of Amparo's death as October 12, the Day of Pilar in Spain, a holiday that celebrated Columbus's discovery of the New World as well as an important feast of the Virgin. I was convinced Amparo died in the predawn hours of the 11th from what Benedicta had been told. When I looked up the 11th on the Catholic calendar, I found it commemorated the Council of Ephesus' declaration in 431 A.D. that Mary was truly the mother of God.

We crested the mountain. San Rafael lay beneath us, the exact place I had been forty-six Julys earlier. I had written an imagined description of this town, and stared eagerly at this touristy mountain retreat. We parked on the same main street I had walked as a child. At a nearby hotel we inquired about Villa Frutos. The owner could not help us, but pointed to where the old civil guard barracks and telephone exchange had once stood, now a park and a bar respectively. Between them, a street swerved east to the railroad station and Segovia. The main road continued on towards El Espinar and Avila.

The brisk air smelled delicious. Well-to-do *madrileños* thronged the cafés and stores. We walked towards the northern edge of town because Conchita had mentioned that the villa was situated on the outskirts. Maruchi was undergoing a similar flashback experience. She told how once, when she and her sister were walking with me and my father, we saw some bulls that had escaped from their pasture. My father said, 'Don't move and they won't hurt you.'

The sidewalk ended. An old woman in black was walking up an alley with her market basket. She detoured with us to a shop where

An old postcard view of the resort village San Rafael in the Guadarrama Mountains north of Madrid. The chalet Villa Frutos, the summer house where we were living when the Civil War began in 1936, would be situated in the upper right edge of the photograph.

Upstairs front window of the chalet Villa Frutos in San Rafael, looking up from under the chestnut tree.

an older woman with tight, grey curls pointed north with the feather duster in her hand. She remembered a Villa Frutos further on. Clusters of wild poppies and black-eyed susans bordered the blackberry thickets at the roadside. The towers of the sanitarium came into view just as we spotted a derelict house almost hidden behind a magnificent chestnut tree. A plaque on the wrought-iron arch over the padlocked front gate contained the faded words '*Villa Frutos.*' We were back to where the nightmare had started on July 18, 1936.

I peered through the bars at the chalet. The second-story windows were framed in red brick. A small balcony with French doors was enclosed with the same curlicued iron that made up the fence. Down the lane, we found another gate, half open and overgrown with brambles. I pushed aside the thorns and Queen Anne's lace. The side door was ajar, inviting me inside.

The passage led upstairs. The stairway was half demolished, rusty nails and broken glass underfoot. Testing each step, I climbed the narrow flight, avoiding roof tiles and fallen plaster. The place felt like a collapsed mineshaft, dark and foreboding. In the upper hallway I saw the roof had caved in.

My sense of Amparo's presence increased. She was the last woman to live here. During the War it must have been used only as a barracks. I looked around, half expecting to find familiar odds and ends, pages of my father's manuscripts. In the hallway stood a half-ruined bureau which I thought I recognized. Could the house have remained vacant since the day we left? I started taking photos and drawing floorplans. A back, central room might have been the living room. The master bedroom behind it contained a rusted-out double bedframe—probably the same bed Amparo and my father had slept in for the last time.

One side room was crammed with a jumble of furniture. Could it have been mine? I photographed each area, working my way towards the front. Then I climbed gingerly downstairs and photographed the view from the back door into a garden next to a stone wall. The main kitchen must have been on this floor because it contained a built-in tiled woodstove. Here Amparo spent her last few days of happiness.

The house had been so overgrown by surrounding trees that it was difficult to take a decent photo of the exterior. Behind it, another gate led to a neighboring house. Below it, the valley unfolded in golds and greens towards the distant mountains. Truly an idyllic spot. I could picture Amparo and Ramón's final walk together to the forest. Across the highway, the meadow rose gradually to the pines. Here, their final parting had taken place.

After my father and the Riveras had escaped, and while the rebel column roared past the chalet, the women quickly gathered Papá's papers and burned them in the stove. Old business cards, envelopes, books, anything that might have given away his political associations. Amparo hesitated over the manuscripts. Wouldn't he be back in a few days? There were some chapters of a new novel and some poems. Did she bury them in the back garden, wrapped in the oilcloth from the kitchen table?

Conchita reported what happened next: "At noon, all the hotels received orders not to serve lunch to the guests because the troops who would be leaving for the capital soon were to be fed first. All the hotels put boards across benches with sheets for tablecloths and the soldiers devoured everything. Then the column began to make its way up the mountain. Above them, the defenders had closed the pass and were waiting to ambush them. Almost immediately the scattered shots we had heard became a constant rattle.

"Celes, the Riveras' cook, came running. 'Airplanes!' she shouted. 'Lots of them from over the mountain!'

"The booming sounds which I had assumed were artillery now became louder and louder. Bombers! Madrid had sent eighteen planes, all they had, to stop the column. We quickly gathered everyone into a downstairs bedroom. Explosions were coming from the center of the colony."

Conchita slapped her thigh. "*Madre mía*, and Emi in the thick of it! We searched for a way to distract the children and began to sing. But in spite of our songs, the noise of the bombs became louder. They fell on the high road with earsplitting concussions. You, Monchín, screamed and held your head. The planes passed over and then returned to the chatter of machine guns. Bullets whined outside the house and we could hear men screaming.

"'We have to leave!' Amparo shouted over the uproar.

"I certainly agreed. Our conversation was interrupted by the whistle and detonation of a bomb almost outside our gate followed by the crash of breaking glass. Naturally everyone was terrified!" Conchita threw up her hands. "They bombed like they never bombed again! My God! And Emi at the telegraph office! The military armed some townspeople who went around shouting that the village had to be evacuated within twenty-four hours. All civilians had to go to El Espinar—men, women and children.

A short while later Emi arrived looking like a wild man. He had come along the river behind town like the Riveras. "There's a terrible battle going on!" he shouted. "All these generals and captains and colonels are going crazy! They are either dead or out of their minds! Let's get out of here!"

"Those final hours in San Rafael were indescribable! The airplanes massacred the column! Those poor little soldier boys had come in good faith, thinking, 'Let's go to Madrid on a military exercise,' because they hadn't been told the truth. And there arose such screams!

"When we evacuated the chalet, there were forty or so dead in the street. We put the baby in the stroller and piled her clothes on top of it. Amparo carried a blanket and I carried another. We didn't know where we were going to sleep or anything. People were streaming out of town, mostly on foot with just the few belongings they could carry. There was no possibility of finding a ride. So out we went, with you, Monchín, screaming '*No quiero ir, no quiero ir!*' 'I don't want to go!' until Dionisia had to pick you up. Emi carried the radio which Amparo insisted we bring because it was our only contact with Madrid and Pepe. Such a strange-looking group we were, but no stranger than others we encountered."

Bleeding bodies lay along the roadside and screams and shots could be heard on all sides. Truckloads of fascists and soldiers roared past while republican militiamen hidden in the woods sniped at them. The merciless sun added another discomfort to the hysteria and panic. The Rivera girls were old enough to understand what was happening and were appalled by all the dead bodies. They had not taken twenty steps when Amparo remembered something— Andrea's rubber bath. Back she went inside and returned with her face chalk-white.

"Moorish soldiers are in our apartment!" she said.

One of them had put on a sweater of Pepe's over his uniform. Moors in Spain again after so many centuries! Memories of the atrocities they had committed in Asturias had made her hesitate, but he only nodded and smiled at her. She picked up the baby's bath and fled.

"So many people were escaping to El Espinar!" Conchita continued. "Many of them would spend the night on the street. I saw society women from the hotels weeping.

"Finally Emi said, 'We're going to the sanitarium. These children can't walk three kilometers to El Espinar!'

"It was where I had gone to talk with Santiago, and Emi knew many of the doctors. We had hardly gone half the distance when a truckload of loyal militia made a suicidal attack on the rebel infantrymen. We all threw ourselves on the ground until the shooting stopped. A driver was killed and his truck overturned down the embankment. Without the servants, I would have collapsed on the spot, but they were brave souls and kept us moving. As it was, I was trembling with terror by the time we arrived at the large iron double gates. Luckily Emi saw a staff doctor he knew.

"'Let us in, for God's sake!' he pleaded. Behind us, others paused to listen. 'The children can't walk any farther!'

"'Look, Emiliano, the military have taken us over as a hospital,' the doctor said. 'We have strict orders not to let anyone in.' He glanced at the children, then over his shoulder before opening the gate. 'Quick, enter! But you are the very last.' The crowd immediately swept forward but he pushed them away and shut the gate. 'No more room!' he yelled.

"'Let us in, let us in!' they shouted.

"One large man with a child in his arms began screaming, 'For the love of God, open the gate! I am the tenor Fleta with my wife and four children!'

"'Sir, I cannot,' the doctor replied. 'Behind you are a thousand more wanting to enter!' He locked the gates. 'There's nowhere to sleep but the garage,' he said. 'The beds are full with the wounded.' He led us to a low outbuilding which stretched the length of the garden and beckoned us inside. 'Lock the doors,' he told us. 'Unless it is I who knocks, don't open for anyone! I hope to God no one learns you are here!'

"The garage was filthy. We only had the blankets we had brought, nothing else. Celes and the servant girls had some of the children's clothing with them wrapped in newspapers. With the blankets on the floor, we were able to put you children to bed, but that night was like one of those horror movies. You cannot imagine what a nightmare it was! It makes me shrivel inside to think about it! You two little ones went to sleep, thank God, but the Rivera girls couldn't.''

Conchita's eyes widened. "Next door to this garage, in the same building, they had set up an emergency clinic. We heard some colonel screaming with pain all night long, 'My legs! They've cut off my legs! Give me morphine or else a pistol to end it!' Both of his legs had been blown off in the bombardment. We passed the whole night hearing the screams from the operating tables and the colonel who begged to be killed." She shook her head sadly. "They were not prepared to care for these men—no anesthesia, no surgical saws to amputate limbs. I'm telling you, it was unbelievable!"

At five the next morning, the same doctor came and said he had found us a ride to El Espinar. Amparo asked if there had been any news of Santiago, hoping for word of Pepe. But no one had seen him. We rode in the back of a milk truck to El Espinar, a small town of workers and farmers. In normal times, they served the rich summer crowd at the village. We were let off at the main square which was packed with refugees.

The mayor and all the town officials were lodging people in private homes as well as they could. He assigned us to a magnificent stone house right on the square, the best in town according to Conchita, beautifully furnished with only a few servants occupying it.

"They put us in a Moorish palace!" Conchita declared. "Such elegant furniture and paintings! Also, we needed more of the children's clothes and went back to the mayor. "*Por Díos*, help us go back to the chalet!" we begged him. It seemed safe enough, now that the fighting was concentrated in the mountains.

"He agreed, but said someone must accompany us because San Rafael was full of military vehicles and soldiers. Without them we wouldn't have been allowed into the area, and he told us we would have to go after dark. 'Two falangists will take you in a car,' he said. So we went at eleven at night, and it is something impossible to describe. Amparo stayed with the children. The Riveras' servant Celes, one of the other girls, and I went for the clothes. Celes also wanted to fetch belongings at the Riveras', but the house was in the center of San Rafael.

"I said, 'Look, Celes, do what you want but I'm not in favor of our going. How are we going to get all the way there?'

"'You're right, *señora*,'" she replied. The poor woman wasn't able to get any of the girls' things.

"However at the chalet it was possible. I always preferred summer homes that were as far outside town as we could find them. We rented that one for six or seven years. But I have never been back. Noooo!" She rolled her eyes. "After that night, I would never put my feet there. I would drop dead on the spot!"

She drew a deep breath. "That night—I can't describe it! Only a marvelous painter could have captured the scene. You don't know what a thunderstorm is like in the sierras. First it gets very hot and then by evening the thunderheads gather. Five minutes after we reached San Rafael, the thunder started and a black cloud partially filled the sky. We had just entered the chalet when we heard the thunderclaps and we said, 'Well, it won't last long. We'll wait. There's only one cloud and it will clear up soon.'

"Then we began to hear all these horses neighing and carrying on. We thought they were cavalry horses, but when we went down to the garden, we saw the most incredible spectacle! I had never seen anything like it in my life! A whole field of horses had broken loose because the fences had been demolished by the bombardments. Look! Over the whole countryside, the road, the horses were going crazy! They were leaping and rearing and carrying on!" Her dark eyes widened. "I'm telling you, it could have been the Apocalypse! Twenty or thirty horses jumping from the fields onto the highway from all sides, neighing and screaming. No one could catch them because they wouldn't respond! They were rearing up like mad creatures with their hooves in the air, insane with terror from so much shooting and so many airplanes dropping bombs!" She flicked open her fan.

"So that was the night of the twenty-third and I said, 'My God, my soul, I will never come back here again!' And I had enjoyed San Rafael a lot because it was so pretty. It wasn't a town—just a colony which depended on El Espinar, but much cleaner and with fewer flies."

Amparo's radio functioned as their major source of news. Madrid reported the workers had overrun the Montaña barracks and armed themselves. The hastily formed militia dispersed into the country-side with great enthusiasm, as if going on a holiday. Untrained, they died by the hundreds with incredible bravery as if to prove their loyalty by dying. Although the insurgent generals had captured about one-third of Spain, the four main industrial cities remained under republican control, and Franco's Foreign Legion was stranded in Morocco. The navy's ships were in the hands of loyal sailors who were blockading the Moroccan ports. The Alto de León pass above San

Rafael had fallen to the rebels, but fierce fighting continued on the other side of the mountain.

In Madrid, the workers took over the city. They painted their union's initials on the cars they expropriated and drove about in a victory mood. Restaurants and hotels were collectivized, mansions of the wealthy transformed into schools and clinics that distributed birth control information. Pawnbrokers were required to return pawned items to their owners because they were seen as preying on the poorest citizens.

On the twenty-fourth, the women took turns going out to see what food they could find. Whatever was available had to be divided to feed a town that had suddenly quadrupled in size. They would ask for a kilo of bread and be given a half. On the other side of the main plaza from the house was the telegraph office. Emi presented himself there, explaining he had no orders.

"Better stay here than on the street," they told him. "There are armed men everywhere looking for trouble!"

On the twenty-fifth at about one-thirty, Amparo was breast-feeding the baby while the servants prepared the meal. Conchita was seated near her.

"They must have arrived in Madrid by now!" Amparo kept saying with an anxious expression.

"Woman, of course!" Conchita assured her. "Santiago knows the mountain like the palm of his hand. Relax, Amparo. After all, you're nursing the baby. When they get there, they'll send you word."

Emi arrived at noon. "You ought to hear the rumors in town!" he said.

Just as he spoke, machine guns began firing outside and everyone jumped to their feet. Emi and Conchita tiptoed out on the balcony and saw townspeople with pistols and some civil guards in the plaza. They were firing at the rooftops and others on the rooftops firing into the street.

"Open the windows! Open the windows!" they were shouting. "Stay out of the windows and balconies!" They wanted no opportunities for snipers.

"You can imagine I came inside at once!" Conchita said. "And your mother went to pieces where she sat. 'They're going to kill us!' she began screaming. I took the baby from her breast and said, 'Bring her a glass of water with lemon!' When it was brought I said, 'Look, Amparo, drink this and we'll prepare a bottle for the baby. For God's sake, calm yourself!' Your mother was having an attack of nerves and her milk would become bad. 'If they kill us, it's our hour to die, that's all.' In these matters she was always very fearful.

"We put her to bed and bathed her face with some vinegar. 'We should do this!' Amparo was moaning. 'Do that!' It was a horrifying situation! Such shootings! *Madre mía*! For three or four hours I believed we were in hell! The heat! The people in the streets all huddled together, not knowing where to go! And people shooting at each other! It was Dantesque!"

"There we were, on the second floor of the house. Just then one of the servants came running in shouting '*Señora*! Militiamen are climbing the stairs with bayonets pointed!' I thought we were all going to die! We didn't even have identity papers! So I picked up the baby and I took your hand. These are spontaneous things of the moment when one does not have time to plan.

"'Leave me here with the children!' I ordered. 'They won't harm them. If they kill me, then goodbye, everyone, but it's the best prospect we have.'

"Holding your hand and the baby in my arms, I walked out to the stairs where the uproar was going on. Seven or eight militiamen with bayonets fixed faced me and I thought, 'This is my moment to die!' I was very frightened but not until afterwards because, to tell the truth, I have a certain serenity at times like these.

"'Believe me or not, but I am the sister of the revolutionary writer Ramón J. Sender!' I told them. 'And these are my niece and nephew, his children. We were summering in San Rafael. The others went on ahead and we became separated.'

"'You're telling us stories!' one of them shouted.

"'It's not a story, boys,' I replied calmly, talking serenely but with tears running down my cheeks. 'I beg you for the lives of these two little creatures. Their mother is killing herself with anxiety in the other room because their father is in Madrid. You must believe me. We were put in this house and don't know whose it is! The mayor lodged us here!'

"Go back! Go back!' the one in front shouted. He turned to me. 'Don't worry, you haven't lied!' Facing the others, he waved one arm. 'Back, back! We'll move on!' To me he added, 'Rest assured, *señora*. No one will enter this house.'

"And I said, 'If you come in, open a bureau and find guns, you'll kill us! But you can't hold us accountable for what you find because it isn't our house! We came here grateful for the beds and the roof over our heads, but we don't know what's here! If you find arms, they aren't ours!'

"And he replied, 'It's nothing, comrade! Don't worry, you're out of danger! I believe what you said, that these children are Sender's. You're really his sister?'

"'Yes, and the mother of these children, my brother's wife, is lying down with a tremendous attack of nerves because she's breast-feeding the baby and doesn't know whether her husband's alive or dead!'

"'Take it easy!' he said. 'I'll put two guards downstairs. No one will molest you further.'

"That moment I felt I had been reborn! This happened around four o'clock. Around seven, the civil guards came back from I don't know where and captured all the militiamen. In that same plaza outside our window, eight hundred militia people—both men and women—were tied up with ropes and machine-gunned—all of them! Because the fascists won that particular battle. At the beginning, many incidents of this sort occurred with the militia. What destroyed them was that they gathered in groups of two hundred or more, armed to the teeth without understanding anything! In San Rafael there was incredible chaos, first one side and then the other gaining the advantage until the fascists killed them all. What these poor militia people did not know was that Segovia, the provincial capital, was already in the hands of the military and well-armed civilians."

The next day, Celes came back early in the morning from searching for milk and bread, whatever food she could find.

"*Señora*," she said to Conchita. "We have been saved by a miracle! The owner of this house is the chief fascist of the town!'

"We can't stay here!" Conchita said. "I was able to convince those militiamen to leave, but another time we might not be so lucky!"

When Emi came home she took him aside. "Listen, this house is a powder keg! You stay while I go talk to someone."

She found the mayor and said, "For God's sake put us in another house because this one is too much responsibility. Give us the most modest place you have."

There was an empty summer cottage outside of town on the road to Avila. Conchita accepted it at once. Although the accommodations were minimal, they were lucky to find anything. Everyone moved there that same day except Emi. So he would not have to walk across town four times daily, he found a room across the street from the telegraph office where he could sleep by himself. Conchita went there to cook him his meals on an open grate with sticks of wood.

She chuckled at the memory. "I had never cooked like this! The little old landlady, very agreeable, said to me, 'I'll do it, *señora*, allow me!' But I said, 'No, no, you will teach me.'"

"You see, the El Espinar telegrapher knew that Emi had married Ramón Sender's sister. He said to him, 'The less you come and go, the better. Someone might see you who knows you and do you harm.'

She shook her head with a mournful expression. "Emi was never able to overcome his bitterness, he even expressed it to your father, that just because he was married to me they would have killed him. He had his own liberal ideas, but politics he never liked. He never belonged to any party. However just because he was married to a Sender, anyone could do him harm. We were put out on the street for twelve years!"

CHAPTER 8

**AMPARO'S RETURN
TO ZAMORA**

ONCHITA leaned back and began fanning herself. "Well, that was the twenty-sixth. Emi and I stayed in El Espinar only two more days because on the twenty-seventh or eighth the order was given that all Communications personnel should present themselves at the military governor's in Segovia within forty-eight hours. This meant Emi had to go, and clearly I wasn't going to abandon my husband!

"Amparo was at the cottage with the children. So I went there— no, I didn't go there—Emi went. He said, 'Look, Amparo, Conchita and I must go to Segovia at once. Take your evening walk with the children and bring everyone to say goodbye.' That's the way it was. Amparo, you Monchín, your nursemaid Aisia, the baby, the two Rivera girls, Celes the Riveras' cook and Adelina their nursemaid— everyone came. They embraced us and I said, 'Amparo, there is no other remedy. You know Pepe is out of danger, because if something had happened we would have heard. But Emi has to go to his post and I'm his wife! If they kill Emi, they take my life as well! I love him with all my soul.' Together we had eighteen hundred pesetas and we kept one hundred for Emi and one hundred for me. I said,

'Take the rest, Amparo, there's nothing more we can do. Besides, they will have to pay Emi on the first.'

"I explained that we would look for a rented room with kitchen privileges, the most economical we could find. Anything above what we needed to live I would send her with a wagon driver or someone. From Segovia to El Espinar is only ten kilometers.

"'Don't say more to anyone than that your husband is in Madrid,' I warned her. 'None of us have documents, so if they ask for his name, say it's José García, a common name. Like fifty thousand others, you have to stay here while your husband is elsewhere.' The mayor also told her that she could buy bread, milk and meat with vouchers available at the city hall."

Conchita seemed concerned that I understood the details of her break with Amparo. No doubt this event had caused her much anguish over the years. I imagined Amparo's dark eyes staring bleakly from Conchita to Emi. Circumstances dictated they part, but she could not help feeling Emi and Conchita were distancing themselves from her for their own safety.

"'Don't move from here, Amparo!' I warned her. 'At any moment the government troops may break through via Peguerinos and put down the rebellion. Tell them who you are and they'll put you on a truck and—*vamos*—we'll all go! Otherwise stay here in this cottage like all the other women.'

"'That day in the big house on the square!' Amparo moaned. 'If you had not been there, what would I have done?'

"'*Por Díos*, Amparo, stay calm above all else,' I told her. 'Otherwise you can't breast-feed the baby. These horrors can't go on forever. Things are so bad they can only improve. But as for us, look how Emi keeps saying, 'No-no-no, we must leave here. They've told me I have twenty-four hours to report or they'll kill me!'"

"I told Amparo, 'El Espinar sends milk to Segovia, and I'll send you notes with the driver. When you find an opportunity, send me a letter.'

"We embraced each other and this was our last farewell. I kissed you all and said to her, 'Don't worry, but be watchful, Amparo!'

"The mayor said, 'We'll send a couple of civil guards with you.'

"'I'd prefer you didn't,' Emi replied. 'The truck's uncovered. If a government airplane comes over and sees the guards in the truck, they'll shoot at us! Commend us to God's care, but without the civil guards.'

"The mayor saw his point. So we left for Segovia in the late afternoon on another milk truck, ten kilometers of anguish with the Castilian sun beating down on our heads. We arrived around seven and Emi said to the driver, 'We don't want a hotel or a pensión.' Probably we wouldn't have found one anyway because Segovia was crowded with refugees. So I said, 'Look, you drivers know people and there must be a modest house where you stay that has rooms to rent.'

"And the driver said, 'Right in my house! Because I'm a man of fifty-odd years and a widower. I have two single daughters and the three of us live alone.'

"It was also near the telegraph office. So I said, 'That's it!' We rented it for a hundred pesetas a month. Emi reported to the military government and to the communications sector which was in a hopeless tangle because telegraph traffic had increased so much.

"The first day he came home from work, he said, 'In the telegraph room there are seven employees and behind us are four fascists armed to the teeth! We have to give them every civilian telegram. They read it, seal it and say, "It stays here forty-eight hours!"'

"Imagine how many families were trying to get in touch, one in one place and one in the other! The third day we were there, our friend the driver came home and said, '*Señora*, the gentleman at the El Espinar telegraph told me to deliver this to you. Otherwise there would have been a forty-eight hour delay.'

"This man must have been a leftist, although he didn't say so. He treated us very well and his daughters also. In the telegram your mother said, 'We are all leaving for Zamora. I will send you news. Amparo.'

"I began to cry because I thought, 'This creature, how can she go to Zamora?'" She began slapping her thigh rhythmically. "'In Zamora everyone knows she's married to my brother! (slap!) And Zamora, like all of Castile, was in the hands of the fascists! (slap!) Ai, this woman!' The El Espinar telegrapher had sent it on the same paper she had written it. I told Emi when he came home that evening, but I didn't explain how I received it. I said, 'What do you think? I'm horrified! How could she do this?'

"'Amparo won't leave because all the trains are paralyzed,' Emi replied. 'Franco has given the order. No trains depart from Segovia except the one that leaves at midnight.'

"It was a troop train carrying soldiers but it had one coach for civilians. A person needed a pass to travel on it and it ran only at night, without lights for safety reasons, moving slowly so as not to make much noise.

"All night long!" She threw her arms upwards. "And in the morning they arrived at Medina del Campo where civilians had to wait all day in a type of barracks!

"The Segovia station was three kilometers from the center of town. 'I'm going,' I said to Emi.

"'But woman, it must be days since they left!' he replied. 'That telegram must have been delayed forty-eight hours or else some sort of espionage is going on and you'd better not tell me about it.'

"So I said to Emi, 'The driver's daughter told me civilians have to wait for days to leave on this train. The station is crammed with people and it's being bombed daily! There's only one coach available. If Amparo and the children haven't been able to get on—!'

"And Emi said, 'But Conchita, it's been at least two days!'

"'Good, I'm going!' I said.

"'I'm going with you!' Emi replied. 'But if someone sees me, that's the end of my job!'

"Then the daughter said, 'I'll go with the *señora*. I've lived in Segovia all my life. Don't worry, *señor*. With me everything will go well.'

"So we went together. The place was crammed with civilians and soldiers waiting for that one midnight train. We asked everyone, 'Have you seen a woman with four children, a tiny baby girl, a two-year-old boy, two girls of four and seven (the Rivera girls) as well as some servants?' No one knew anything. Someone said, 'With luck they may have left the same day they arrived.' The station was in total confusion with people seated on the floor, but no sign of Amparo. We looked everywhere. The station people said, 'Look, it was night! There were so many people! Between signing safe-conducts and arranging tickets, we don't have time to notice anyone!' So we returned to the house and a few days later they transferred Emi to Burgos. We left Segovia in the same train Amparo had taken but in the opposite direction."

However Maruchi Rivera remembered that we spent a few days in a recently constructed house in Segovia. It was empty of furniture, and the women collected fruit crates at the market which they used as tables and chairs. Although it was summer, the nights were cool and it was hard to sleep. Conchita, not knowing where we had taken refuge, had accidentally missed us.

Amparo could not have imagined things worse elsewhere than they were El Espinar, the constant artillery in the mountains, the random shootings in the streets. Worst of all was the dreaded sound of airplanes overhead and the bombings. The children's terror and Guadarrama's occupation by the rebels on August 1st convinced her to follow her husband's advice: Go to Zamora, the provincial town where life never seemed to change. If she waited much longer, her dwindling cash reserve wouldn't cover the train tickets.

From scattered conversations in the station waiting room, the women learned that German transport planes were ferrying Franco's legionnaires to Seville and Cádiz. Obviously the rebellion was not going to end in a week, perhaps not even in a month.

From Zamora, moreover, it would be easy to cross into Portugal with the help of friends. There she would take a boat and join Ramón's brother Manolo and his wife Marcelle who were vacationing in Biarritz. She looked forward to seeing her family, especially Antonio, her younger brother. It was through him that the radio had come into their lives, even before the telephone. His handmade receiver had connected them to all of Europe. Saturnino finally had allowed him to place one in the café as well as in the living room upstairs. When Antonio built a short wave set, he could tune in more distant stations. One day he rushed in excitedly to say he was receiving Russian broadcasts. The whole world seemed to be beaming information towards Zamora.

In Segovia there were occasional air raid alerts. The railway station was a favorite target for republican aircraft. One day two bombs dropped on the tracks but did not explode. Armed men patrolled the streets or lounged in groups beside doorways, some in army or Carlist *requeté* (conservative monarchist militia) uniforms, others merely wearing armbands. We ate meals in a nearby café, waiting in line to order what little was available.

"Eat, eat!" my nursemaid Aisia ordered us. She pantomimed devouring a mouthful of food and we copied her with exaggerated gestures.

At last Amparo secured tickets and travel passes. The women packed up their few things, wrapping the radio in newspaper and twine. Evening had fallen by the time we settled ourselves on the train platform for the long wait until midnight. Amparo thought once more of phoning the telegraph office and leaving a message for Conchita but decided it would only increase Emi's anxiety. She talked to Celes of her sympathy for the man. He was living his life braced against the expected blow, the exact attitude that invited someone to strike. Far better to throw out your chest like Ramón and behave fearlessly, Amparo said. Not only did this discourage the cowardly aggressor, but made life worth living. How hard she was trying to cultivate a similar attitude!

Because of us children, we were given seats on the train. It arrived in Medina del Campo at dawn and all civilians en route to other destinations were ordered to remain in a warehouse which had been transformed into a barracks with cots and mattresses.

"But we have to eat something!" Amparo insisted. "Can't we go to the café?"

"No, only to the bathrooms. A man is coming from the station tavern and you can order from him whatever he has. The train won't leave until eleven or twelve tonight."

Faced with a twenty-hour wait, the women made themselves as comfortable as they could, chatting with other travellers. Madrid Radio reported the rebellion had been contained and Amparo's spirits brightened. When the man from the station café came to take food orders, she recognized him as a friend of Saturnino's. For days she had been thinking of telephoning Ramón. The early hour was an ideal time because he would be asleep at the apartment in Madrid. Or so she hoped. When the café owner approached them, she introduced herself and asked if she could place a long distance call.

"Of course, *Señorita* Amparo!" He beamed happily because she had remembered him. "It's strictly against orders, but bring the baby as if you need to wash her. Things are so disorganized, how is anyone to know?"

The armed sentry outside the door allowed her to pass with the baby. In the café, she settled herself at the end of the bar with the phone and a cup of strong coffee, Andreina gurgling on her lap.

She dialed the operator. "I wish to call Madrid."

The woman made some comment about 'priorities' but Amparo, from her years with the phone company, was familiar with their procedures and explained it was an emergency. There was a buzz, a loud click and a man's voice came on the line.

"Yes?"

"Ramón? Oh, at last!"

"Whom do you want?" The voice was suspicious and unfriendly. Amparo's hopes faded. "I'm calling Ramón Sender in Madrid."

"Why are you calling Madrid?"

"Because I'm trying to deliver a message to my husband, for the love of God!" All the days of agony spilled over in her voice.

"One moment please. Stay where you are." The line went dead.

Amparo shrugged. Were the lines tangled? She jiggled the hook. "Operator?"

"One moment please."

A few moments later, an army vehicle pulled up by the door. Two uniformed men approached her.

"*Señora*, you are under arrest," the lieutenant said.

Amparo was terrified. "What have I done?"

"You are suspected of espionage," he said. "We intercepted your call to the other zone."

"But I was just calling my husband! You mean it's not possible to phone Madrid?"

"You were attempting to contact the enemy," he replied. "All such calls are monitored and investigated."

"But—!" Amparo was dumbfounded. "May I at least inform the others travelling with me?"

They accompanied her to the warehouse where she explained to the women what had happened.

"I had no idea I was doing something wrong!" she said to the officer. "How long will I be gone? I am breast-feeding my baby."

He gave an exaggerated shrug. "Bring her, but we must leave at once."

With a despairing look at Celes, Amparo shouldered Andreina and started across the crowded room.

I read the panic on Amparo's face and ran after her screaming, "Mamá! Mamáaaaa!"

She bent down to me. "Monchín, it's all right. I have to go away for a little while but I'll come back." She glanced up at Aisia who was hurrying towards us. "You stay here."

I was not convinced. The soldiers frightened me, and I could sense Amparo's distress. "Mamáaa!" I howled, struggling to free myself from Aisia's grip. She had to carry me back kicking and screaming.

Amparo was taken to an army barracks and ushered into the

presence of a young colonel lounging behind a desk. He stared at her before beckoning her to a hard-backed chair. The other two men took posts beside the door.

"Name?" he asked.

"Amparo Garcia." She arranged the baby on her lap and glanced at her questioner briefly before swinging her gaze towards the window. "Colonel, I used to work for the phone company. I didn't realize I was doing anything wrong."

"We have to investigate all calls across the lines, *señora*." He picked up a sheet of paper. "You attempted to contact a certain Ramón Sender in Madrid. He glanced up at her. "What is your relationship to him?"

Amparo realized she would have no opportunity to use a false identity. "I am his wife," she admitted. "I was trying to let him know where we were. My children and I were in San Rafael when the trouble began. I'm taking them home to my family in Zamora." She tried to meet his gaze with a frank expression in spite of the terror she felt. "That's all there is to it."

The colonel tapped a pencil on the blotter. When he smiled, one large front tooth gleamed rabbit-like between his lips. "A simple error of judgment, you say, but do you have any proof?"

She looked down at Andreina. "What can I offer you? I have four women and four innocent children in my care." She flung him a haughty look. "For God's sake, *señor*! If I was a spy, would I travel with eight people? My family in Zamora can vouch for me."

The colonel called his assistant. "Get Zamora on the line, will you?" He turned to her. "Who are your relatives?"

She gave them Saturnino's and Magdalena's names before being led to a bench in the anteroom. The muted voice of the colonel penetrated through the door, and idly she wondered with whom he was talking. When she was ordered back into his presence, he was standing by the window, hands clasped behind him.

"Saturnino Barayón has been detained," he said. "I was unable to contact your other relative."

Amparo was astounded. "Saturnino? But why?"

The colonel shrugged. "We are in a state of war, *señora*." I must keep you here until this matter is cleared up." He crooked a finger at the guard. "Rest assured that you and your child will be fed and properly treated."

Saturnino in jail! Dazed, Amparo allowed herself to be led to a cell in the back of the building. Up until this moment, she had not doubted the wisdom of Ramón's advice that she return home. Could the terror have spread even to Zamora? The jailer, a courteous civilian, brought her a meal. Later in the day, when it became obvious they would detain her through the night, she asked that Monchín and Aisia be brought to visit but was refused.

In the morning, she gave the colonel the phone number of her half-sister Casimira as well as the names of the most influential, conservative people in Zamora she could think of. At midday, she was once more brought before him. He informed her that Miguel Sevilla, Casimira's husband, was willing to take responsibility for her release. She was returned to the station but tagged as someone to be watched.

Her reappearance was greeted with tears of joy. Celes had taken charge in her absence and bought food until her money ran out.

"We have been living like gypsies!" Aisia said. "And Monchín never once stopped asking for you."

My happiness was boundless. I caught her skirt and held it tight to make sure she would never leave me again. "Mamá, Mamá, stay here!" I repeated over and over.

The train's scheduled night departure from Medina del Campo must have been delayed until just before sunrise. Sections of track had been bombed the previous day and had to be repaired. Although daytime travel was risky, the military situation in the south required that vital equipment and personnel be sent at once. An armored locomotive was backed into position, its boiler protected with hastily welded steel plates. Obviously the commander was gambling that Madrid's impoverished air force could not mount bombing raids two days in a row.

Amparo squeezed up against a window, the baby on her lap. I shared Aisia's seat beside her. The aisle was full, people seated on the floor or on their suitcases, balancing the coach's sway by holding onto armrests or each other. All the women were on the verge of exhaustion. It had been days since they had been able to bathe. Amparo mentioned how there was always a good supply of hot water at the family apartment because of the café on the ground floor.

What should have been a two-hour journey took all day because of frequent stops for military reasons and the constant threat of bombing attacks. Finally we crossed the Duero River, and the town of Toro loomed on the cliffs ahead. Amparo stared at it with vague

curiosity, remembering childhood outings to the annual wine celebrations. The train hooted twice, running along the river on the final
leg of their journey. Two minutes later, the brakes were applied so
suddenly that people in the aisle toppled like dominoes. The whistle
continued sounding a series of short blasts.

"Out, out!" the conductor shouted. "Air raid! Hide yourselves
below the embankment!"

A panic-stricken rush for the exits began. Afraid the children
would be trampled, Amparo held back until a whiskery grandfather
gestured for her to precede him.

"Women and children first!" he said.

Others took up the phrase. "Women and children!" The jam in
the aisle loosened and the car emptied. Pepi began to cry. Maruchi
Rivera watched her with the superior air of a six-year-old who had
outgrown such childish behavior. Outside, soldiers were helping
passengers down the slopes. To the south, the distant hum of approaching airplanes could be heard. Pepi and I began screaming in
earnest.

"Quickly!" A fierce-looking officer shouted. "Down the hillside!"

Amparo slid on her haunches, the baby against her chest. Aisia
and Celes each held one of Pepi's hands. A large culvert which could
hold a dozen people lay under the track bed.

"Over here!" A hunch-backed youth gestured at us from inside.
He huddled in a ball, hands over his ears with his mouth open to
lessen the concussion of the bombs. "Like this!" he shouted.

The sound of the airplanes diminished over the cliffs only to return with the first explosions. They were flying low, parallel to the
river. With the whistle of the descending bombs, Amparo clutched
both of us, her back towards the culvert opening. An enormous blast
knocked us backwards against Celes and the girls. Smoke and dust
filled the tunnel, making it impossible to breathe. Everyone began
backing towards the uphill entrance, choking and gasping for air.
Another bomb exploded on the cliff above, sending an avalanche of
dirt and debris tumbling down. Two women had run out the uphill
side and were half buried.

We lay together on the culvert's curved slope. It was easier to
breathe within the enclosed space Amparo's encircling arms created.
Celes and Adelina were trying to soothe the girls. More bombs were
dropping in the distance, but the worst seemed to have passed.

"Don't go out!" the youth warned. "They will come back and gun us down!"

His words went unheeded by several hysterical women who ran downslope towards the river. The officer peered into the culvert. He spotted the two women moaning on the other side and yelled for the medics.

The harder Amparo tried to escape the demon of war, the closer he came. San Rafael had been nothing compared to this! The youth's advice proved correct. The bombers returned to machine-gun the coaches. Bullets sent rows of dirt skyward and tore foliage from the poplars. They pinged and whined from the steel armor of the loco-motive and punctured holes in the coach windows.

At last they were gone. Once more death had passed us by. Not so with others, because soldiers were carrying bodies wrapped in blankets towards the coaches. Repairs took several hours before the train, travelling at a crawl, limped the final few miles into Zamora. The rebel commander had badly miscalculated Madrid's determina-tion to disrupt rail traffic.

We arrived in Zamora in the evening. The most picturesque ap-proach would have been from the south across the ancient Roman bridge with guardtowers. Instead we arrived via the northern out-skirts where the station was located. Fourteen days after her flight from Villa Frutos—and six years after her departure from Za-mora—Amparo had finally come home. Why had she not visited before? She had become such a different person in Madrid, more so after she met Ramón, and she had not wanted to face her relatives' criticisms. Antonio was different. As far as he was concerned, she could do no wrong.

Half an hour later, the women pulled up in front of the family café in two taxis. But the doors were shut and there was a 'Closed' notice in one window. At this hour? The café remained open every day of the week!

"What's wrong?" Amparo asked the driver.

He shrugged. "The *dueño* was arrested. He's in jail in Toro."

Of course! Biting her lip in anguish, Amparo peered through the plate glass. Someone was inside and she knocked loudly. Andrés, the teenage son of the cook Señora Gregoria, glanced up from mopping the floor. He came to unlock the door.

"Amparo! What are you doing here?" He glanced behind her at

the women unloading the luggage. "Nati and Magdalena are up-stairs. You'd better go up. I'll bring everyone inside."

"Where's Antonio?" she asked.

"Both brothers are in jail," he said. "The café's closed indefinitely."

"Antonio too?" Amparo dug her fingernails into her cheeks, transfixed with horror. "How can it be?"

"Zamora's in the hands of the *falange*," Andrés whispered, his eyes scanning the street. "Get inside quickly. It's best you're not seen."

White-faced, she explained the situation to Celes and the others. "Wait for me in the café," she said. "I'm going to find out what's going on." She handed the baby to Aisia but I would not leave her side. Rather than risk my yells, she took me with her. I insisted on climbing the stairs by myself.

Amparo's half-sister Magdalena answered the front door. In her mid-forties, she was a dignified woman with a square-cut chin. Amparo treated her more like an aunt. Beside her stood her eleven-year-old daughter Magdalena (nicknamed 'Nena' by the family), Amparo's niece, who exclaimed delightedly when she saw us.

"You should not have come," Magdalena said. "But now you're here, child, come in." She smiled at me. "I thought I would never meet your little ones."

"There are six more of us downstairs," Amparo said. "The train was bombed—we've been through hell." She leaned weakly against the wall. "What about Antonio and Saturnino?"

Magdalena's bloodshot eyes testified to her weeping. "They took Saturnino first and Antonio a few days later. It's been a very bad time with many arrests." She turned to her daughter. "Nena, bring the rest of them upstairs."

Amparo described the turmoil of her existence since July 18th. "Finally there was nowhere else to go." Her self-control collapsed and she began to weep helplessly. "It's been too much, first one thing and then the next! Everything's been indescribably horrible!"

Upon seeing her distress I began to whimper and tug at her skirt. "Mamá, Mamá!"

She looked down at me. "The worst has been the effect on the little ones." She bent down and cupped my face in her hands. "It's all right, Moncho," she soothed. "Mamá is tired. Come on, let's take a big bath!"

I sensed her anguish over her brothers and stayed close to her that evening, refusing to go to bed unless she remained beside me. The fearful events of the journey had suffocated my spirit. Also the food in Medina del Campo had upset my stomach. When I fell asleep, Amparo sat by her radio to listen to the local Salamanca station. Little Nena, delighted to see her aunt, leaned against her holding her hand.

The announcer's voice interrupted the music of a *zarzuela*. "Five shiploads of Foreign Legion troops have arrived from Morocco, and General Franco has flown to Seville to establish his headquarters." There was a burst of martial music. "France has announced a policy of non-intervention and proposes it be adopted by all of Europe."

Amparo switched it off. How could the French socialist premier Blum have betrayed the Republic? It couldn't be true! Otherwise why was she trying to escape to Biarritz? She tried not to think about it. At the dinner table, she found her fingers trembling so much she could hardly get the fork to her mouth. At last she pushed her plate away. "I can't eat," she said. "I feel like I'm caught in a nightmare."

CHAPTER 9: INTERVIEWS IN
ZAMORA

O N my return to Spain I repeated Amparo's journey to Zamora from Segovia. "When you go to Zamora, be careful with whom you talk," I had been warned. "There are no middle roads. There are only those who gave the blows and those who received them. Many times those who are guilty will say no, they are not. And if Miguel Sevilla is alive, say to him 'I am the son of Amparo Barayón and I have come to find out how and why she died.'"

The flat landscape gradually changed to foothills. Beyond them, a sloping mesa punctuated the horizon. We clattered on a trestle through the treetops to the north bank of the Duero River. On the cliffs ahead appeared Toro, the town where Amparo's brothers were jailed. Zamora, Amparo's birthplace, lay beyond the violet evening haze. Now, in spite of the warnings I had received, I would find out the truth.

We were met by my first cousin Chori, Magdalena's younger sister, and her husband. Her close-cropped salt-and-pepper hair matched mine, a solidly built woman with a strong chin and deep-set eyes. Her husband was balding, his square face beginning to settle towards his neck. Both seemed more than a little nervous.

Over *aperitifs* at the apartment, Chori brought up her concern that names should not be mentioned in my book. "The guilty ones are dead," she said. "The children should not suffer for their parents."

"Who were they?" I asked. "We heard a certain Viloria—"

"Yes, Viloria was the one who shot Amparo. But Miguel Sevilla, married to my Aunt Casimira, also must bear some responsibility. He could have saved her because he was friendly with the *falange* and connected to the Church. Also, Casimira taught French to the sons of the military governor Claomarchirán."

Sevilla. Magdalena mentioned him in her first letter to my father. "Why didn't he intercede on Amparo's behalf?" I asked.

"He was fearful."

"What happened to him?"

Chori shrugged. "They moved to Seville and are no longer alive. The rest of us held them in disgrace."

Would I have preferred him to come to some violent end or to have lived out his years in full knowledge of his guilt? Too late, I had come too late! Whatever dreams of vengeance I might have harbored, of confronting those responsible, I had to forget.

"Viloria died insane in a mental hospital," Chori added. "He was despised by everyone. For so many years we knew nothing about you. Then one night we heard your father on a radio program and he spoke of you and your sister. We were so happy to know you were safe in America! Magdalena wrote to him at once. The second time we wrote was when Magdalena was imprisoned."

"We knew nothing about this!" I exclaimed.

Chori described how Magdalena had been denied entrance to the University of Salamanca in spite of excellent grades because two uncles and an aunt had been shot as communists. Soon afterwards, she was jailed for two years. Her father wrote Papá and told him what had happened. Papá replied saying she should get out of politics because it was a filthy mess. He had seen his political ideals become meaningless. He also said that we children had not been told what had happened to our mother.

Magdalena phoned to say she could not join us. Couldn't we travel to Málaga instead before they left on vacation August 2nd?

"Listen, we never knew you were in jail! Chori just told us."

"See what you can do about coming here. I'll call again."

Later we took a quick drive past the family café, Café Iberia, now a restaurant, on the edge of the *Plaza Mayor* a half-block away. I gazed at Amparo's childhood neighborhood, the church of San Juan where she had played the organ. I had imagined all of this. How incredible to be seeing it at last! Darkness was falling by the time we registered at our hotel.

That night I dreamt of a tower full of statues that came alive when I touched them. I was two people in the dream, he who animated the stone effigies and he who discovered them. A blissful mixture of terror and awe awakened me. In the darkness I reinvoked the feelings by recalling the dream.

The next morning, the family took us on a tour of the city. Another fine day awaited us with rows of clouds similar to yesterday's. We roamed the interior of the cathedral which overlooked the Duero River from the southernmost cliff, late Romanesque with a Byzantine dome of overlapping curved stone shingles. I preferred the sunlit gardens we passed on the way to the cathedral museum.

Later, we walked the parapet for the view south. At the *Plaza Mayor* we strolled to San Juan's, Amparo's church, where she had sung and taught catechism. It was fenced off for repairs, the interior inaccessible. We continued to St. Vincent's Church where Benedicta had been baptized for the second time after Amparo was jailed. The religious ladies in town did not believe her "communist" mother had seen to it in Madrid.

We drove to the building that used to house the orphanage where my sister and I had stayed. It had been renovated into a state-owned hotel called a *parador*. I walked the polished hallway whose floor-to-ceiling windows surrounded the central courtyard. Nothing looked familiar except the stairs which for some reason drew my attention. Something about them—walking up? Falling down?

Next morning, we walked with Chori towards the Plaza Mayor for a round of interviews. Near the café, we passed an acacia-like tree in full blossom which gave off a luscious perfume. Its scent and the shrill cries of the darting swallows overhead evoked a memory. As a twenty-two-month-old child, I had smelled this exact smell.

That day I received one of the best photographs I found of Amparo. She looked about sixteen, her hair in pigtails, her face three-quarter profile over a wide plaid collar. I recognized my sister in her large, deep-set eyes and the length of the face above the slender neck. It was an extraordinary portrait that captured Amparo's artistic sensibility and character.

Amparo at approximately sixteen.

Dionisia Diaz Cortes, known in the Sender family as "Aisia," the young niece of the building manager María Cortes. Aisia was hired by Amparo to care for Monchín. Here she is pictured with the little boy she cared for in Zamora after Amparo was jailed.

We also visited the couple who had hired my nursemaid Dionisia after Amparo was jailed. Like everyone we had met, they were extremely hospitable.

The wife described how she had employed Dionisia because she needed a nursemaid for her son. "She stayed almost two years with us and spent most of the time weeping. She would return from a prison visit to Amparo and cry her eyes out. It's not possible for someone to cry more than Dionisia cried for Amparo. I never have seen a better brought up, loving person at seventeen years of age. She read every newspaper and book we had."

She brought out a photo of a moon-faced, attractive girl with a pageboy cut. The little boy on her lap was about the same age I was when I knew her.

Something about her was familiar. "Aisia," I whispered. The name pulled my mouth into a smile. A happy name for a loveable girl.

"This girl was someone very special," the wife repeated. "She was a person, I don't know, of such great kindness. She used to say, 'You're like my parents. Keep me with you.' When we heard later what happened to Amparo, we all suffered because Aisia loved her so much. She sang her praises constantly! We had Amparo's suitcase in our house. It contained photos, clothes, shoes, a large comb. I remember it well because our boy always wanted to open it and Aisia refused, saying, 'This suitcase is sacred to me.' She often rearranged the things inside it. She kept it impeccable. But whenever she did this, she would put her head on the table and weep."

"Then one day some men came asking for her," the husband added. "'We've come to reclaim the children,' they said."

"Dr. Junod of The International Red Cross?" I asked.

"We didn't know," the wife replied. "So I went to the kitchen and told her, 'There are some men here asking for you.' Aisia came out sobbing and they said to her, 'We're here searching for the children.' *Ai Díos*, what a day for the poor girl! She went off with them and came back late crying. She went to bed in tears because they were taking her Monchín and she wasn't able to see him." She leaned towards me. "If one day you meet her, everything I have told you is nothing compared to how she felt. She was crazy about your parents, and even more so about you children."

"How old would she be now?"

"Sixty-two or three."

We must find her when we returned to Madrid. And what happened to Amparo's suitcase? Dr. Junod must have given it to my father.

During two more days of interviews, I began to wonder if my cousin Chori's presence might be inhibiting people from speaking freely about the family's involvement in Amparo's arrest or their later actions. I had told everyone I was writing a book. Could I blame them if they tried to present themselves in a sympathetic manner? But I was committed to this approach. Maybe Magdalena would set things straight. Suddenly I realized how every one of our informants had been a woman. The tragedy of a mother's sacrifice was never forgotten by other mothers. They saw with their hearts the true dimensions of the human drama. Historians, usually male, have chronicled the glorious combats. But it was the anguish of families which enshrined the true saga of humanity.

On Friday I awakened determined to spare the relatives more efforts on our behalf. I could not pressure Chori to do more than she had been doing, but still had discovered nothing tangible about why my mother had been killed. No one wanted to tell Amparo's son the more gruesome aspects of the story. The ten days I had scheduled for Zamora were drawing to a close. Perhaps I should hire someone to continue the search.

That afternoon we broke away from the family and visited the Socialist Party's local headquarters. All indications pointed to a socialist victory in the October national elections, the first time since 1936. Everyone wondered whether the army would attempt a coup. The local deputy to the *Cortes* welcomed us warmly. He offered us his help and set up an immediate appointment with a Señora Chillon.

Señora Chillon lived over a clothing store owned by her son Ángel, a tall, stoop-shouldered man with El Greco-like features. He took time off from his customers to usher us upstairs. His mother greeted us in a V-neck dark blue dress with white polka dots, her face a foreshortened version of her son's.

"My husband Manuel Antón was the first man shot here in Zamora," she said. "He was a well-known socialist."

The lines alongside her mouth were deeply etched by suffering. Obviously she was devastated by her husband's death. She never would forgive or forget his martyrdom.

Ángel returned from the telephone to join us. I photographed mother and son standing beside a bust of the father on the dresser. Then she read a few stanzas from "The Jail Of Zamora," a poem which she wrote in 1936:

Sad eyes, fastened
From the doorway on the jailer,
With what yearning you wait
To learn if he whom you love still lives!
You fear the worst. Your anguished glance
Is fixed on the door,
Waiting for the notice to be posted
That you should pick up his clothes.

Yours is the distant stare
Of someone too fearful to ask
If he who is detained there
Needs something you could bring . . .

His clothes are handed to you
In silence. The jailer says nothing,
Not meeting your gaze.
The signal is infallible.
The prisoner is no longer alive!

When mothers, daughters, wives
Receive clothes like this,
They emit such terrible screams!
Why doesn't the earth tremble under them? . . .

Against your bosom you embrace
Clothes which no longer will cover
That beloved body
Which filled your home
With love and hope,
With light and work and bread.
In them his life still resonates
With all its ardor,
Allowing you to feel
His presence next to you . . .

The intensity of her recitation wove a spell, her words the outcry of a tormented spirit. I was deeply touched because she spoke for those uncounted thousands of Spanish mothers and wives whose suffering had never been told.

Ángel listened quietly to her voice. It surprised me he was not more embittered. I could be him, I kept thinking, if Amparo had lived and they had shot my father instead. The doorbell rang and Señora Chillon broke off. Ángel returned with Dionisio, a man in his seventies, grey hair slicked back above bifocals, his face taut with excitement.

"At last we meet!" he shouted. He walked over to embrace me vigorously and plant kisses on my cheeks. "I was the last to see Amparito alive! I was in jail also, and my job was at the front desk where they checked prisoners in and out. I was there when they brought Amparito downstairs on the way to the cemetery. She said, 'The last moment of my life I dedicate to the memory of my chil-dren!' Those were her exact words!"

I made sure I was understanding him correctly. "You heard Amparo say this?"

"She left with those words on her lips!" Dionisio repeated even more emphatically.

I was stunned. Face to face, finally, with the last person to see her alive except for her killers, I had nothing to say. I imagined a frosty October night in Zamora. A squad of uniformed men hurried a lightly clad woman through the prison corridors towards the court-yard where a truck was waiting.

"Amparito was my friend!" Dionisio shouted. "I knew all the girls at the telephone office!" He embraced me again and grabbed my arm. "I was the last one to see her alive! Ángel, phone Lolita! You know her number!" He turned to me. "I will take you to meet Lolita and Pepita who worked with her!" He squeezed my elbow. "I remember Amparo coming to my father's fish store! She carried her baby and wore a white dress!" He was a charming fellow, full of good will and a desire to help, but overwhelming. "When is the best time?"

"I'll phone you tomorrow," I promised.

In the nearby village of Coreses later that evening, I met a grey-haired workman in a coverall. "Are you Ramón Sender Barayón?" he asked me. "I was talking with friends about your visit, and they said, 'Don't forget to tell Ramón Sender's son that it was he, Claomar-chirán, who denounced his mother!' Raimundo Hernández Clao-marchirán was the military governor responsible for the daily lists of men and women 'released' from prison to the death squads." He leaned back, his eyes half shut. "That's all I have to say."

"At six in the evening they arrived at the jail to select those they were going to shoot," someone added.

The man nodded somberly. "One of Claomarchirán's grandsons once accused his own father. He said, 'How could my grandfather have lived, and you also, with the knowledge that you both have so many deaths on your heads?' The father grabbed a pistol to kill his son, but the cook intervened. 'How can you shoot the boy?' the cook shouted. 'He's only twenty years old!'"

Miguel Sevilla as Judas, Raimundo Hernández Claomarchirán as Pontius Pilate and Segundo Viloria as executioner, the cast of Amparo's passion play was now complete. All three were dead.

That same evening I was introduced to a young grade school principal named Fernando Primo. He had been working on a thesis involving some of my father's novels. The longer I talked to him, the more convinced I became that I had found the right person to continue researching Amparo's story after I left. We made an appointment to meet the following day.

Saturday morning: Walking with Dionisio, once more I passed my favorite tree and inhaled its perfume. A tendril of memory connected me to when I had walked here holding my mother's hand. We turned into the street of the café—*Trascastillas* was its old name, "behind the castle." Now it had been renamed in honor of a local sculptor.

"The only diversion we had when we were young was to take a short walk," Dionisio said. "It was hard for girls to get permission because they led a very cloistered existence, like little nuns. They were not permitted to go out for coffee or take a walk with a man. We lived like primitive anthropoids!" He pointed to an appliance shop. "The telephone office was right there!"

How small Amparo's world was! She lived her early years in almost a one-block area. In the café I explained to the plump patroness that I would like to photograph the work areas and dining room. She agreed, and I began. Faces turned from the stove to stare in curiosity. In a side room, tablecloths were drying on clotheslines. I caught a glimpse of the back alley whose exit onto the square had served as a shortcut for the Barayón children.

The patroness said something to one of her kitchen staff. He returned holding a heavy china cup inscribed "Café Iberia." She handed it to me, a memento of my visit. I was delighted because I had never owned anything Amparo touched. She might have drunk from this very cup. I imagined a dark-eyed, animated twenty-year-old woman laughing at a table or standing behind the cash register. Or perhaps the muted notes of a Chopin nocturne would be filtering through the ceiling from where she was practicing in her room.

"I met your mother when she was twenty years old," Dionisio told me. "My wife and her sisters went to the same school. They were neighbors."

I had an appointment with my possible researcher Fernando at the Valderey Café. Dionisio bade us farewell after setting up a meeting for tomorrow.

Fernando was waiting with his wife and their four-year-old. I discussed a business arrangement: he would continue researching Amparo's life and I would send him a small monthly retainer. I asked him to help us locate several possible informants including my nursemaid Dionisia

That evening we joined friends for a farewell supper at Pozo's restaurant next door to the old family café. Throughout the meal I kept thinking how, in a paradoxical way, I was the host because we were eating in the very house where Amparo grew up.

After dessert I ordered a round of cognac and made a toast. "It makes me very happy to be here with you," I said. "To share a meal in my family's house." I paused to try to find words in Spanish to express what I was feeling. "I would like to offer a toast to the memory of Amparo. Our being here together is the best tribute we can give her."

Eyes sparkling, they all raised their glasses. What if I had spent my life here with Amparo and her family? Amparo would have been upstairs at this moment reading a story to her grandchildren while I entertained guests from afar. It could so easily have happened.

I said goodnight to the owner Señor Pozo and asked if we could return tomorrow morning and photograph the family apartment upstairs. Poor man, he could not refuse.

The next day Dionisio accompanied us to the apartment of the two Muñoz sisters whose mother had been Amparo's piano teacher. The older one explained how, like Amparo, she graduated from high school and went to work for the telephone company.

"Amparo was one of us," she said. "Our mother loved her very, very much. She didn't want to teach piano to Lola here because she said they would come to blows. So she said, 'Amparo will give classes to Lola.'"

"She gave me classes in solfège," Lola explained in a husky voice.

The older sister told how she studied French with Casimira, "The half-sister who married Miguel Sevilla, *el sastre* (the tailor)."

"*El desastre* (the disaster)," Judy commented, a good Spanish pun. "He could have saved Ramón's mother."

The sisters looked nonplussed. "Miguel Sevilla?"

"He identified himself very closely with the Cause!" Dionisio yelled. 'The Cause' was a reference to the fascists.

"I believe the real cause was . . . " The older sister hesitated. Again we were in that area of silences that spoke louder than words. "Eh . . . the terrible fear that occurred everywhere . . . even in the other zone there were things like this . . ." She drew a deep breath. "Amparo was a different person from her brother Saturnino, completely different! She was a woman who took daily communion!"

"But why was it that Sevilla, if he was so religious, did not involve himself in saving Amparo?" I asked.

"This is hard to comprehend," the older sister replied. "Because no one really understood Amparo Barayón, frankly, because when they told me what happened . . ."

"No, no!" Dionisio shouted.

"You saw what happened!" Lola added.

"I saw it!" Dionisio exclaimed.

"When your mother died, how old were you?" Lola asked me.

"Almost two years."

"And where did you live?"

"In the orphanage." I stumbled over the last word in Spanish.

"Well, let's pin it down." She turned to her sister. "Don't you really believe someone known to Amparo Barayón would have taken charge of the boy?"

"No, because they wanted to hide it!" Dionisio exclaimed.

"We were not told! No, no!" Lola cried.

"Because they were inhuman!" Dionisio added.

"No, no!" the sister insisted. "If they had told us something, my mother and my father would have been the first to have claimed them! No, sir!"

"There were the sisters of his mamá, Magdalena and the others! Did they know?"

"I think the family was very fearful," I said.

She shook her head. "I firmly believe that my mother, knowing her as I do, would have said, 'Amparo's boy will stay with us!' She wouldn't have let a moment pass without bringing you here."

"And the baby girl! The baby girl!" Dionisio said. "She was still being nursed when they took her away and killed her mother!"

The conversation turned to how Amparo was denied absolution after her final confession. Both the sisters didn't believe the story. According to them, there was no way the priest would not have absolved her. He was an intimate friend of their father.

"How ignorant you are!" Dionisio shouted. "Excuse me, but I know how these things were done! I worked in the prison office! I detested that man! He was responsible for many bad things. Because of this I don't want to discuss him."

I explained how a highly placed cleric begged my sister's forgiveness on behalf of the Church during her visit to Spain because of this priest's actions.

"That's right," the older sister replied. "I remember he was disciplined and transferred to a bad position before retiring. He lives in a small village far from here. Paradinas. He's probably almost ninety years old."

Our time was running out. Dionisio walked as far as the Plaza Mayor where he embraced us with great warmth. His eccentricity probably protected him better than a bulletproof vest during the Franco years. When we arrived at Señor Pozo's, he was just returning home with an armful of groceries. His face fell at the sight of us. What traumatic memories did we evoke? I reminded him of my request to photograph the family apartment. It was a very personal demand to make of a Spaniard, but he could only agree.

I took both color and black-and-whites of the interior. The hallway was paved with five-color octagonal tiles which had survived since Amparo's time. Out the back window I took a shot of the jumbled rooftops. These also had not changed, I thought. Amparo had stared at this same view. All my senses were turned up full because I had spent some weeks here with her. These walls echoed her excited, girlish chatter, and the music of Granados and Albeniz she played on the piano. How many similarities existed between her life and mine! Throughout my teens I practiced piano three or four hours a day, no doubt many of the same pieces.

Which room was hers? I was hesitant to open doors because Señor Pozo seemed so nervous. I satisfied myself with the kitchen, hallway and living room. No doubt he thought I was wondering how he came to inherit the place. I assumed that when the government confiscated everything, they auctioned it off to the highest bidder.

I could elect myself judge and jury. I could play out a Sicilian vendetta fantasy and track down whatever person still survived who had been even distantly implicated in Amparo's murder. What if I demanded an admission of guilt—from whom? A doddering priest whose senility could only awaken my compassion? I had come too late. Amparo's murderers had remained in power for forty-odd years, long enough for the world to have turned its attention to fresher atrocities.

We thanked Señor Pozo and walked down the Calle de la Reina behind the apartment to tour the neighborhood. A block away I photographed the old city wall and the nearby building which once had housed the family ice factory. It too had been auctioned off as "war goods" and now had become a hardware store.

So far, my breakaway from the family had not brought me any closer to the truth. People had talked more freely of Sevilla's role, but that was to be expected. I had collected the names of others who made up the execution squad with Viloria—Sebastián the druggist, Mariscal the postman, but nothing more. What else could I find?

I had to keep reminding myself that no matter what I found or how much I heard, Amparo would remain a shadow. Nothing would bring back her voice, her laughter, her touch or smell.

The following morning we went to the Civil Registry with Ángel Chillon to search for Amparo's birth certificate. We were walking an upstairs corridor when a man dressed in a suit approached us. A dignified type in his late sixties, he greeted Ángel with a nod and a word.

"That is Hernández, the son of the military governor Claomarchirán," Ángel whispered. "As a young soldier, he delivered the execution lists signed by his father to the jail."

Claomarchirán's son! What a strange feeling, passing him on the way to verify Amparo's birthdate! I should have stopped and introduced myself. What could I have asked him? "Did your father know, when he signed the prison release for my mother, that it meant her death?" "Were you the person who delivered it?" I would be the last person to whom he would speak openly. What must it have been like for those who had to live in such close proximity with the men guilty for their relatives' deaths? A parallel situation in America could be found in the South where black families resided in the same town as the Klansmen who had lynched a father or uncle.

At the Civil Registry we gave the approximate year of Amparo's birth to the clerk. He hauled out one leather-bound register after another, running his finger down the columns. In 1907 her younger brother Antonio's name appeared. At last he found her, born on May 8th, 1904. That meant she was thirty-two when she died and not twenty-nine as I had estimated. I accepted an official copy and we returned to the sidewalk.

"Where is Claomarchirán's son's office?" I asked.

He shrugged. "Not far. Just a few blocks."

I decided to pay the man a visit. It was my last opportunity before we left town to confront someone at least indirectly involved with the guilty ones. But I wouldn't tell Angel because he had to live there. We bade goodbye to our friend and five minutes later rang Hernández's doorbell. A maid ushered us into a well-appointed apartment and a book-lined study. The man behind the desk, white-haired with a clipped mustache, looked every inch the prominent attorney.

"May I be of service?" he inquired.

"I am the son of Amparo Barayón," I explained. "I have been told that you might be able to verify some facts regarding my mother's death."

"Amparo Barayón," he repeated, gazing thoughtfully at the ceiling. "That name is familiar. Was she Casimira's sister?"

"Yes, that's correct."

He nodded with a smile. "I know her name because Casimira was my professor of French. But I did not know her personally."

"She was arrested and shot in 1936," I continued. "One version of the story reports she was detained for insulting your father the military governor."

He spread his hands and shrugged. "Of this I know nothing. Perhaps it is possible but so much time has passed."

I tried again. "She was the wife of Ramón J. Sender, the novelist. I am here to find out if this was the reason she was murdered." His open gaze protested his ignorance, yet something did not ring true. I was convinced he knew more, but what could I do? "Would you permit me to take your photograph?" I fully expected him to refuse, but he seemed flattered by my request and agreed. Would he have done so if he had something to hide?

Afterwards, there was nothing left to say. My wife had noticed that the books on his shelves included numerous official histories of Franco Spain. This meeting would be the closest I came to confronting anyone even distantly responsible. But as Chori asked me, must the children pay for the sins of their parents? Even if as the military governor's son this man had carried the death lists to the prison, could I accuse him of complicity? Every attempt I had made to pin down concrete facts about Amparo's killers had ended in frustration. Either people did not want to mention names or else the passage of so many years had dimmed their memories.

That afternoon we returned to the Plaza Mayor to talk with Waldo, a poet and flamenco scholar we had met. From an outdoor table I watched the wind rustle the three flags on the city hall, Spain's, the province's and the city's. Zamora, Zamora! As the old saying went, "You don't win Zamora in an hour." Amparo's story also could not be won in an hour, a week—or a year.

The bells rang out a hymn. Everyone was taking their stroll, the street crowded with walkers, young married couples with their children, teenage boys cruising in tightly bunched squads. Waldo came to join us, a grey-bearded man with a kindly face.

"*Hola, amigo!*" I called.

"In all honesty, I deeply sympathize with you but I cannot help you in your search," he explained with ornate Spanish courtesy. I will try to find you someone who knows more." He raised his voice to override the motorscooter revving beside us. "The story of your mother is one of those incomprehensible things. Your father was connected with the anarcho-syndicalists, but your mother was a religious woman!" He pointed across the square. "She taught catechism in that very church! She came home thinking that because she knew everyone there would be no problems, and instead went to her downfall without knowing why." He shook his forefinger. "Without knowing why because she had not participated, according to what everyone knew, in any political movement. Naturally she had her sympathies for this or that idea, but she was never an activist in any sense of the word."

He sighed and smoothed back his hair. His features were so similar to mine that we could have been related. "You see, we felt great hope when World War II finished. Everyone thought the Allies would open Spain." He leaned forward. "And no one opened anything! They sold us down the river!" He glanced at a squad of young soldiers strolling past. "We called ourselves 'The Accursed Generation' because we were all under lock and key. There were those who were imprisoned, those who were orphans, those who were drafted in the Blue Legion and forced to fight for Hitler on the Russian Front—and us. Imagine!"

Pedestrians swirled about us. If only I could have reached into their minds and filtered out what each one knew about Amparo! All the information I needed was passing before me in the memories of these people.

"Was anything ever published about the killings in Zamora?" I asked.

Waldo shook his head. "Unfortunately not. An interesting fact is that when this current opening occurred, this liberalization, those of the Right had a terrible fear that we would hit the ball into their court—that we would take vengeance. But the reaction of the Spanish people has been fabulous." He stared at me. "You must hear this, Ramón, because this is the great lesson the Spanish people has to offer you."

Waldo was telling me Spain had put away the nightmares of the past. Here there had been no Nuremberg tribunal to judge the guilty and satisfy the victims of this particular holocaust. Of course there still existed those individuals who could not forgive and forget, who played the loops of their personal tragedies over and over. I myself ran the risk of becoming one of these, of endlessly cycling on the theme of Amparo's death. My father during one of his return trips said: "I can forgive the fact that my wife was shot but I cannot forget the deed. Only God can forget such an act; man's nature forces him to remember."

CHAPTER 10

THE BETRAYAL AND
ARREST OF AMPARO

I HAD heard many opinions and theories, but in the end I gathered the following facts:

A few days after Amparo arrived in Zamora, she and the other women were brought in for questioning and then released. However Amparo had announced her intention of applying for a passport to leave for Portugal. That, plus the fact that she was known to be the wife of Ramón J. Sender, the radical author, resulted in her being placed under a type of house arrest whereby she had to sign in at the police station daily. She remained at the family apartment with the two of us and Nati, her neurasthenic older sister. Magdalena, her husband and eleven-year-old little Magdalena lived just across the street. Meanwhile, the Rivera girls and servants moved into the small cottage of the waiter Andrés and his mother who cooked in the café. Every day more and more people were being arrested. Magdalena was in anguish because her husband expected to be imprisoned. Fascist execution squads were dragging people out of their houses. Mutilated and bullet-riddled bodies were being found along the roadsides and in the river.

Little Magdalena, or 'Nena,' remembered watching the adults burn books and papers in the café one evening. They also burned a statuette of a woman with a Phrygian cap, the symbol of the Republic. Her mother found a list of local Communist Party members hidden in Amparo's piano. Antonio was a communist and in charge of the archives. We children watched our elders in astonishment as they searched frantically for incriminating items.

Two women friends visited Amparo. They found her seated by the radio. Although it was forbidden, she was listening with great excitement to a broadcast from the other zone. The announcer had reported things were going well for the Republicans and Amparo was euphoric. She was very animated and spoke in a great hurry, a temperamental sort. The war would end in four days, she told them.

When they left, she accompanied them onto the landing and continued talking. Her guests walked downstairs but she shouted after them, still very agitated, "No, no, the uprising will be over almost at once! We are winning!"

"Oh my, Amparo shouldn't be talking like this in public!" the women said to one another. "Because if they hear her—"

The government confiscated the café, the family ice factory and Antonio's electric shop as "war goods." Magdalena was advised to renounce her Barayón inheritance so that her husband would not also be fined.

According to Amparo's younger sister Eugenia, Amparo was arrested on St. Augustine's day, (August 28th), the same day they killed her brother Antonio. "She went to protest what they had done to Antonio. She took the baby with her because she knew they would not harm her with the child in her arms. Then suddenly she understood what they were like in there and left on the run. She understood she had not shown proper respect to the governor and had to escape. On the street she fell. They grabbed her and took her to jail. People later felt the governor had the option of noticing or ignoring her action. If she had left tranquilly—"

But Magdalena told a slightly different version which was confirmed by Palmira who as a fifteen-year-old shared Amparo's cell: Amparo had asked her brother-in-law Miguel Sevilla to use his influence to help her acquire a passport. On August 28th he contacted her.

"Amparo, the military governor wants to talk with you about your request," he told her. "But don't take the baby when you go down."

"But I always take her wherever I go," she replied. What a strange thing for him to say!

"There is apt to be a long wait and—well, I just thought I'd mention it," he finished lamely.

His tone of voice convinced her to do just the opposite. With my sister Andrea in her arms, she started down the block in the late afternoon.

"Amparo!" Her half-sister Magdalena hurried up to her. "Oh, Amparo! Antonio has disappeared! They were transferring him along with twenty others to the Fermoselles jail and they never arrived. Someone reported seeing many bodies in the fields outside Toro."

Amparo was dumbfounded. "You mean they just took them and . . ."

"When they disappear like this, it can only mean one thing." Magdalena moaned, wringing her hands. "Oh God! I've got to talk to Casimira. Maybe Sevilla told her something."

Dazed, Amparo walked the six blocks to the provincial office building, now under the administration of the military. Ushered into Colonel Hernández Claomarchirán's office, she stood with the baby in her arms while he stared at her.

"I spoke with your brother-in-law regarding your application," he said. "Because of the unsettled state of things, we are not issuing passports at present."

"Are you also the one who authorizes the transfer of prisoners?" she asked.

"Yes, but why do you ask?"

"Because my brother Antonio disappeared today while being transferred to Fermoselles."

Claomarchirán spread his hands helplessly. "Ah, these matters are tragic but there is nothing I can do. According to reports I received, all the prisoners involved in the transfer have been found shot."

Antonio murdered? Amparo drew herself up, eyes blazing. "I feel it is my duty, sir, to inform you—" She took a deep breath—"that you are—all of you—vile murderers and scum!" She spat the epithets at him. "I hold you personally responsible for his death!"

Realizing that her fury had bested her, she turned and ran out, slamming the door behind her. She had to get away! Andrea clutched to her chest, she walked quickly back to the apartment. Dionisia had just begun to feed me. Amparo joined us at the kitchen table, breast-feeding Andrea while staring bleakly out the window. Dionisia went downstairs to the café to do the laundry, leaving me dawdling over my bowl of farina. When Andrea fell asleep, Amparo put her down in her bedroom before returning to retake her seat.

In *The Five Books Of Ariadne*, my father wrote of how the sun still shone upon her childhood paradise, but the streets had been invaded by shadows, shapeless forms which she could only see out of the corners of her eyes. As a girl she would have laughed at these dark ghosts, but now they threatened to engulf her.

After weighing all my informants' versions, I reconstructed the following:

A hammering at the door jolted Amparo upright. "Open up! Open up!" a gruff voice shouted.

Throwing a crocheted dark blue shawl around her shoulders, Amparo undid the latch. A police sergeant forced his way past her followed by three men with rifles. They searched the rooms, staring briefly at Nati semi-comatose in her bed.

"*Señora*, you must come with us," the policeman said. "We have an order for your arrest."

"But my children—"

"Leave them." He seemed nervous. "Come along now."

I clutched her skirt, wailing. She murmured soothing words and tried to lead me into the hall, but I threw myself down, arms thrashing.

Hands grasped her arms and lifted her. "Monchín!" she screamed.

She was half-carried to the waiting car. Behind her, I was climbing down the stairs bellowing.

"I can't abandon the children!" she shouted. She leaned out the window. "Dionisia! Magdalena!"

The policeman faced her from the front seat. "*Señora*, as a suspected Red you are without any rights whatsoever." He shrugged. "You should have thought of this before having children." He said something in a low voice to the driver who burst out laughing.

In the laundryroom, Aisia heard Amparo's shout and ran outside just in time to see the car turn the corner. My screams echoed from the landing where I had fallen and cut my lip. She picked me up and brought me upstairs.

At the police station, Amparo was placed in a holding cell with a wooden platform for a bed and a slop bucket. The rationale for her arrest was that she was implicated as a relative of Saturnino and Antonio, and that she had a clandestine radio transmitter in her possession.

The following morning, she was brought upstairs and told they were transferring her to the prison a few blocks away. Prison! Her breasts ached with milk for her baby! She gazed wildly about her, searching for a way out. She waited until both policemen were occupied and then flung herself out the door.

"Halt! Halt!" The shouts were followed by gunshots.

She ran towards the apartment. In front of the post office, her toe caught in the cobblestones and she fell. Half-stunned, she lay there, pain searing her forearm and knee.

Footsteps. She was seized by the elbows and dragged to her feet. "Got her!" the policeman yelled. "Now don't try that again!"

Later that morning Dionisia took Andrea to the prison because Amparo was breast-feeding her. A café neighbor in Zamora saw Dionisia return with me from a visit to Amparo, both of us crying.

Eugenia, who lived in nearby León, left for Zamora immediately. "When I arrived at the apartment, you were seated under a little table screaming in outrage. Your fits of anger lasted such a long time that my mother took you to a children's specialist and he gave her some medicine for your nerves. You had seen many bombardments in the previous weeks. After two or three days, your mother's aged aunt Maximina took you to her farm in the village of Perdigón. Dionisia could not remain responsible for you because she was a minor.

"Maximina was an old woman and half-blind. But she and her husband were childless and delighted to have you. You were sickly—you didn't want to eat, but you ate very well for her. At her house there were chickens and a pig, a garden with a well and fruit trees. You would call for her, '*Tía, Tía!*'"

While I stayed with Maximina, Amparo endured the hardships of Zamora's prison. Two women who knew her there—Palmira Sanjuan and Pilar Fidalgo Carasa, lived to tell of her fate. And because of the literary fame of my father, their accounts were later printed in newspapers and magazines. Together they provide a collective testimony of horror.

Palmira, whose father and brother both were shot in Zamora,

later was sentenced to a long prison term for distributing pamphlets condemning Franco. "I met Amparo when I was jailed with my mother. She had long dark hair, very thick, which she twisted into braids to keep clean. I was a youngster of fifteen and Amparo treated me as another daughter. She was very loving to me. I always wanted to hold the baby and feed her, but Amparo wanted to be with her as much as possible. I was only able to hold her when Amparo had something else to do. I was always saying, 'Amparo, Amparito, give me the baby!'

"All I know about Amparo's story is what she told me. She always accused an in-law named Sevilla. 'It's my uncle Miguel Sevilla who is guilty.' These were the exact words that came out of her mouth. Amparo said, 'He told me to go pick up my passport at the Civil Governor's office. And the strangest thing was that he told me not to take the baby along. Why did he not want me to take Andreina?' These were her exact words! She talked with my mother about it.

"Sevilla was friendly with all the killers. He knew who had been condemned to die and when they were going to be shot. Amparo always said, 'Sevilla is the guilty one!' She named him just like that. He knew days ahead that they were going to kill her.

"Amparo did not care for her family because none of them concerned themselves with her situation. They brought her none of the things that families usually supply to their loved ones in jail, no soap, nothing! There was only one person who came to visit her, a young girl who was in service to your family. She brought her sandwiches and was always weeping. She was the only person who cared after Amparo in prison. She brought her a little soap occasionally.

"Amparo's family did not behave well. Normally, the moment a loved one was arrested, the mothers, the sisters, the children went to the door of the jail to weep, to find out news, to try to see who was inside. They did not visit Amparo. They abandoned her when she needed them and for this they should feel remorse. But not Amparo's husband. If they had captured Ramón Sender—hah! They would have cut him into tiny pieces! Poor man, he had to escape.

"They killed Amparo because they could not kill him. I'm very sorry I wasn't able to talk with him just to tell him he shouldn't feel guilty. Amparo always said that she loved him very much. There was a lullaby she sang to her baby. 'The words were written by my husband,' she said. 'And I put them to music.'

Palmira described how Teresa the jailer brought coffee around eight. Then the women went to the patio where they sat on the ground. Those who had soap washed their things in a large basin, but soap was as precious as gold. Amparo did not put the baby's things in with the other clothes. Instead she washed them in a small bucket to avoid infections. Bathing facilities were primitive, and some of the older women never bathed. They wanted to hold Andrea but Amparo would not let them. She was very kind, very loving, but said no. But Palmira would sit down and Amparo would put the baby on her lap.

"Don't get up or you'll fall with the baby!" Amparo would say. She used these moments to comb her hair and retie her braids. The prison provided combs and powder because of the lice. After the midday meal they were locked up. Late in the afternoon they descended to the patio and waited for supper. The men cooked the food over a wood fire in the kitchen. The lentils or other beans were brought in a large kettle and the women lined up for a bowl apiece. After the meal, they returned to the cell and awaited the hour of the "*La Lista Negra*," the Black List which named those condemned to die.

Palmira remembered another mother with a baby in the jail who was named Pilar Fidalgo Carasa, "a lovely woman with blue eyes. They jailed her right after she gave birth and her tiny newborn baby was with her. She was well-known in Zamora because her husband started reclamation proceedings and succeeded in having her moved to the republican zone. Your father could have done the same but he was unprepared. He could have gone to the French embassy and given Amparo's name and perhaps reclaimed her."

During the first period of the war, many persons who found themselves caught "on the wrong side" of the conflict were switched across the lines via the intervention of the Red Cross or a foreign nation. Prisoner exchanges were also accomplished and, in theory at least, Papá could have applied to have Amparo brought out to France.

Pilar later described conditions in the prison: "On my arrival in prison I was compelled to climb a narrow, steep stair-case to a cell already holding thirty-five other women prisoners. I was left there in a half-fainting condition until, under the pretext of being interrogated, I was obliged to climb up and down this staircase several times a day. Because of my recent confinement and my weak state, this brought on a severe hemorrhage and a descent of my uterus. Also I contracted a bladder infection that totally prevented me from urinating. I had not been allowed to bring any clothing for myself or my child, and since there was neither mattress nor coverlet, I had to sleep on the cement floor—even when winter came, and the climate of Zamora was one of the most rigorous in Spain. I tried to wrap up my child so that she would not suffer too much. The temperature in our cell fell below freezing, and her hands and face turned blue with cold. I had only a piece of blanket which a companion had given me to protect us from the bitter cold. Because I continued hemorrhaging, I constantly begged the warden for help. Finally she brought the prison doctor Pedro Almendral who merely came as a matter of form. Upon seeing my suffering, he commented that 'the best cure for the wife of that scoundrel Almoina is death.' He prescribed nothing—neither for myself or my baby.

"The warden, Teresa Alonso, was nicknamed 'the Hyena' by the prisoners. Her daughter was secretary for the Falangist Party, and because of this Teresa had been hired as supervisor of the women prisoners. She insisted we address her as '*Doña* Teresa' while treating us with brutality and overwhelming us with the grossest offenses. In our presence she insulted our husbands and seized every opportunity to be cruel. Her helper Ludivina was serving a life sentence for infanticide.

"The prison regime was barbarous. Two days after my arrival I gave up trying to breast-feed my baby, because all these emotions had dried up my milk. Every afternoon I was given only a little cup of goat's milk and water. The child had to drink it cold, for we were not allowed to make a fire. I was attempting to coax her to drink the evil-smelling liquid from a baby bottle when the Hyena entered the cell.

"'You don't know how to be a mother!' she shouted, and pulled my daughter from my arms.

"She thrust the bottle so violently into the baby's mouth that the baby, unable to breathe, turned blue and began to suffocate. I fainted on the floor. When I came to, I was surrounded by my companions. Meanwhile my baby, freed from the claws of the warden, went into convulsions. Not surprisingly, she later fell ill of dysentery and bronchitis.

"One child died of meningitis in our cell. He cried piercingly and died without any medical attention. The day after, both the mother and grandmother were shot.

"At times we were forty prisoners in a cell built to accommodate two people. There were two benches, each capable of seating three persons, and the floor to sleep on. For our private needs, there were only three chamberpots. They had to be emptied into an old rusty cauldron which also served for washing our clothes. We were forbidden to have food brought to us from outside, and were given disgusting soup cooked with soda ash which kept us in a constant state of dysentery. We were all in a deplorable state. The air was unbreathable and the babies choked many nights for lack of oxygen. We were not allowed to go into the yard to dry our washing, so we had to spread it out on the cement floor of the cell. Then we all squeezed ourselves into a corner so as not to walk on it. We tried to soften the heart of the warden and begged to be permitted at least to place the babies' linen in the sun. She replied that we could dry it on our bodies. That is what we had to do, so that the infants should not suffer from wet clothing.

"To be imprisoned, according to the rebels, was to lose all individuality. The most elementary human rights were unknown and people were killed as easily as rabbits—indeed more easily, because to kill a rabbit a hunting permit was required. But to kill people you only had to go into the street and fire on them as a diversion."

Palmira: "In other towns it wasn't like in Zamora. The military revolted and that was that. They arrested people certainly. They killed someone here, they beat up someone there. But in Zamora they shot twenty or thirty every night! They should be covered in shame for everything they did.

"It didn't matter if you were pregnant or not. Engracia del Río was eight months pregnant, a schoolteacher. She came upstairs with two others and they said, 'Go see Don Justo.' Don Justo asked her whose baby she was carrying. 'Mine!' she replied. 'Come on, it's what's-his-name's,' he said. 'I'm not going to say,' she said. A few days later they shot her, in full knowledge of her condition."

Pilar: "The first three women murdered in prison were Engracia del Rio, Carmen N., a beautiful seventeen-year-old with lovely black hair, and María Salgado, a widow and mother of a seven-year-old boy. These last two were led to the cemetery by a band of falangists who, once there, told them to run. If they succeeded in escaping, their lives would be spared. The two women were shocked but, urged on by the instinct of self-preservation, they ran madly from tomb to tomb, jumping over graves and hiding behind crosses and little chapels. Meanwhile the falangists, young *señoritos* of good families, pursued and fired at them as though on a hunt. Wounded, bleeding, victims of an incredible madness, the two women fell dead from the bullets of their hunters. The *señoritos* roared with laughter and recounted their exploits at the casino. On the following day, they took communion at their parish church where the priest impatiently waited to congratulate them on the zeal they had shown in defense of 'Holy Religion.'

"Every day a new and frightful trial began at twilight. With growing horror we watched night fall, wishing the sun would never set. At eight or nine o'clock we all began saying goodbye to one another. Some tied up their belongings in what scraps of material they possessed and used them as a pillow. Some already had given away their jewels, earrings, wedding rings, religious medals to their relatives through the bars of the interview cage. One can guess with what emotion these belongings were received, as well as the final messages for those soon to be orphaned. Others who had not been visited turned over their souvenirs of happier days to those among us whom they thought would be the last to be killed.

"Herminia de San Lazaro, a young married woman and a great beauty, was held prisoner until the month of October. When they released her, she fell seriously ill, either because the suffering she had endured had weakened her or because of the emotions she had undergone. Then they accused her of having thrown a statue of the Inquisitor Diego de Deza into the river. For those who had reestablished once more the Holy Office of the Inquisition, that was a double crime. The clergy and the bigots would not rest until Herminia was dragged from her sick bed and again imprisoned. She entered our cell at dusk and for three hours was prey to intermittent convulsions. That same night they took her to the cemetery and murdered her. She was killed to avenge an offense against a block of stone, the statue of the most infamous among Spain's inquisitors. For a long time thereafter, persons considered to be of the Left were obliged to search in the river for the statue. The searches were in vain, and many of the people drowned.

"For mothers who had a baby with them—and there were many—the first sign that they were to be executed was when their infant was snatched from them. Everyone knew what this meant. A mother whose little one was taken had only a few hours left to live. These were heartrending scenes. For the last time the condemned woman pressed her little one to her bosom and covered her with kisses. It was necessary to wrest the child away by brute force. Then the tears ceased. The woman fell into a state of semi-consciousness, of frightening silence, losing all contact with her surroundings. Many were led to their death in this condition, and it happened almost every night. In frozen stillness we heard the first steps in the corridor, and tried to discover within those treads which of us would be chosen to die that night. Then the door opened. Civil guards and falangists appeared. To hear the list better, we held our breath and, so that our children would not cry, we gave them the breast. They read out the list very slowly—with a tortuous slowness. With the calling of the first name, terror seized us all. Those called gave their bundles to us, and asked us to see their family received it. Those who once more had not been named uttered a sigh of relief at the twenty-four more hours of life assured them, a small concession that seemed such a precious gift. We who had to stay behind, fearing the murderers would prolong their stay amongst us, begged the condemned ones not to delay their dressing. They knew, and we knew, that they were about to be killed. We all were anxious that the scene should end, because when the victims delayed, the executioners hurled the grossest insults and threatened to take us all. Tragically, the unfortunate ones about to die understood this very well and so went quickly, some even without their shoes. However long, however full of change my life will be, neither I nor any of the survivors shall ever forget those moments.

"In the province of Zamora they murdered about six thousand people, six hundred of them women. Bodies appeared on the roads, in the meadows, in the fields, under trees and in the thickets. Some were left as they fell, others disinterred by animals from hastily dug graves. Widows and orphans had to hide their grief for fear of being killed. They begged in secret, because anyone who helped the survivors of a 'Red' exposed himself to being shadowed. Only the Social Assistance organization could officially allay material needs, but only by imposing moral suffering. They obliged the orphans to sing the songs of their fathers' murderers, to wear the uniform of those who executed them, to curse the dead and blaspheme their memories."

Serie AF   № 374651

MINISTERIO DE JUSTICIA
Registros Civiles

CERTIFICACION LITERAL DE INSCRIPCION DE ____DEFUNCION____ (1)

Sección ___3ª___
Tomo ___98___
Pág. _____
Folio (2) 16

REGISTRO CIVIL DE _____Zamora_____
Provincia de _____Zamora_____
El asiento al margen reseñado literalmente dice así: ___REGISTRO CIVIL DE
ZAMORA.=En la Ciudad de Zamora a las once horas y –
minutos del día once de Octubre de mil novecientos
treinta y seis ante D. Agustín Pérez Piorno, Juez –
municipal y D. Mario Aparicio de Santiago, Secreta-
rio, se procede a inscribir la defnción de D. Amparo
Barayón Miguel, de 29 años de edad, natural de Zamo-
ta, provincia de id. hija de Antonio y de Dª Isabel
domiciliada en Madrid, de profesion empleada y de es
tado soltera, falleció en el día once del actual a –
la-y, minutos a consecuencia de, según resulta de...
y reconocimiento practicado, y su cadavez habrá de re
bir sepultura en el Cementerio Municipal de esta –
Ciudad.= Esta inscripcion se practica en virtud de
consignandose ademas.= habiendola presenciado como
testigos D. Argimiro Sobrino Hernandez y d. Francisco de Asis Iglesias Lopez, mayores de edad, y vecinos
de esta población.= Leida este acta, se sella con el
del Juzgado y firman el señor Juez, los testigos de e
certifico.= Agustin Perez Piorno.= Argimiro Sobrino.=
F.Iglesias Lopez= Maria Aparicio.= Rubricados y sella
do.—
           Lo inserto concuerda con su original a que me
remito, caso necesario; y, para que conste y a peti-
ción de parte interesada, expido la presente.—

Amparo's death certificate with an error in her age (she was 32) and listing her as "single." Cause of death is not given.

CHAPTER 11: **AMPARO'S DEATH**

A T the beginning of October, the ground froze and northern Spain's bitter winter set in. As the skies darkened, so did the climate in Zamora's prison. And for Amparo, the worst was about to begin.

Pilar: "One of the most sinister nights I spent in prison was October 9, 1936 when the greatest number of my friends from Benavente were killed. Along with many others whose names escape my memory for the moment, they shot Epifanio Rodríguez Rubio, Felipe Martínez Abad, Ildefonso Lopez, Enrique Villarino Santiago, Francisco Fernández, Luciano García Guerra, Marcelo Carbajo Lora. There was the son of a cobbler named Burgos who was only nineteen years old, Feliz Vara, the painter Ibañez, Alejandrino Perez, Teofilo Infestas and Venancio Alonso. The wife of the last-named, María Garea, was imprisoned with us. The men spent the whole night shut up in the chapel which also served as a torture chamber for the condemned. From our cell, grouped around the poor wife, we heard their cries and screams. Then they came to take María Garea to accompany her husband. I was present at this scene and shall never forget her charging us with the welfare of her two small boys. But worse was to follow. She was taken to the chapel where, along with the

139

others, she found her husband. We heard them moaning as they embraced for the first time since their imprisonment, and also the last time because the moment of meeting was to be the moment of parting. At dawn their bodies, clasped to each other, were thrown into a common pit.

"It was in the same chapel that all the prisoners heard Mass. Throughout the ceremony we had to kneel without turning our heads towards the area of the chapel where the men were. During the long sermon, the priest frequently insulted us by calling us 'Red bitches.' Behind us, our jailers kept guard. In this dismal spot, which had been the scene of so many martyrdoms and sufferings, we found small pieces of paper with a few words of goodbye written by feverish and trembling hands, a last vow or a final request. On the floor and against the walls were splashes of blood. Sometimes, although not without incurring great risks, we could gather up these papers and carefully preserve them."

Palmira: "At six at night they took the men out. I don't know how because I never saw the men's part of the prison. They put them in the chapel next to our cell where we could hear them calling, each one saying things about himself so that we would know who he was. One time my mother thought the voice was my brother's and almost fainted because he was shouting, 'Mother!' Every night there were these dramas, with the men calling their final messages to us.

"Later, when the tower clock struck midnight or one o'clock, they came for the women. From the bottom of the spiral staircase they called out the names of the women they wanted. When someone resisted coming down, they went upstairs. Each one went according to her manner, some bravely, others tearfully, others talking of their father and mother, brothers or children. At that moment they spoke of the persons they loved the most in the world. They went downstairs and what happened to them we didn't know. If the killers told others and these others spoke, then we would hear something. But no loved one really knew how the chosen ones died or how they were killed. If you knew, you were an accomplice."

Pilar: "The story of the Flechoso sisters is no less moving. Angelita was fifteen, her sister eighteen. It tore one's heart to see those two young girls, so ignorant of the fate awaiting them. We did not think there would be any executions that day because generally they did not come on Sundays for victims. Also we wanted to persuade ourselves that no ill would befall the two children. We advised them to rest and make a bed on the floor out of clothes and rags we loaned them. They slept in each other's arms and we watched over their innocent sleep. But towards nine o'clock the executioners came to look for them. Upon hearing her name called, one girl, very gentle in appearance, asked what it meant.

"'Angelita, if you do not feel well, lean on me,' the older one said.

"Together they dressed quickly. We were so upset we could hardly say goodbye. We listened to them descend the staircase and then, as they realized what awaited them, we heard their cries. The following day we heard they had been killed together, clinging to one another. A month later, an order came to set them free.

"I also remember some young girls of the Figuero de la Torre family. Serafina and Aurelia, along with their mother María, were still in the women's cell as if they were dangerous criminals when I was released. A brother, 17, had been killed but the family did not know about it.

"All the members of the Flechas family, both men and women, were killed, a total of seven persons. A son succeeded in escaping, but in his place they killed his eight-months-pregnant fiancée Transito Alonso and her mother, Juana Ramos. In Transito's case, even after she was dead the baby kept moving and they shot through her body many times."

Palmira: "The next day the nuns came to teach us catechism and to love God. 'They killed Transito last night,' they said. 'Shall we say an Our Father for her?' 'Ah, did they?' someone replied with much sarcasm. 'Good, good!' In general I grew to hate nuns.

"Those few months were the worst. They were killing mothers who had small children, even old grandmothers. It was excruciatingly painful emotionally. The fishsellers Juana Ramos and Emilia were both over eighty years old. They were foul-mouthed old ladies and joked about everything, although they knew that in spite of their age they were going to be killed. 'So who are you taking to old Cacabel today?' they would ask the Hyena. But after her daughter Transito was killed, Juana fell silent until the day they called her name. When they took her away she kept crying, 'I have children who love me! Why do you kill me if I have children who love me?'

Pilar: "They did the same with the family Carnero; the mother,

*Palmira Sanjuan Misis, who as a young girl was impris-
oned in the women's cell with her mother and Amparo.*

Pilar Fidalgo Carasa, author of "A Young Mother in Franco's Prisons," and whose testimony in El Socialista *described conditions in Amparo's prison cell in 1936. Photo by Eva Soltes, Mexico City, 1987.*

two daughters and the fiancé of one were all killed. A tailor named Silva, well-known in Zamora, was shot along with his wife. I could cite many families who were completely annihilated.

Palmira: "Many priests acted very badly. The bishop of Zamora in 1936 was more or less an assassin—I don't remember his name. He must be held responsible because prisoners appealed to him to save their lives. All he would reply was that the Reds had killed more people than the falangists were killing."

Pilar: "A priest heard the confessions of the condemned and accompanied them to their execution—not as a devout duty but in the spirit of collaboration. Statements were taken from the prisoners and were the occasion of fresh arrests and executions. I recall in this connection that a priest took it upon himself to speak with the prisoners. By his insidious questions this cleric extracted names and facts which he conveyed to the falangists. He even employed this procedure with those soon to be shot and whose fear and nearness to death inevitably inclined them towards religion. Another priest was the one who said Mass. All his sermons were inflamed harangues against the 'Reds.' He covered the republicans with insults and said that we were not to be killed because we were robbers but because we were connected with men just as infamous as thieves. His imprecations were terrifying, and the most terrible curses came from his lips during the Offertory. He refused absolution to Amparo because she refused to declare that her husband was scum."

Meanwhile, Conchita and Emi had heard of Amparo's arrest.

Conchita: "A month after Amparo returned to Zamora, we were transferred to Burgos. They put Emi in front of the telegraph key, but there was almost always a guard. He waited until one day at three in the morning when they were less busy than usual and the guard was on a break. Then he wired his Zamora comrade that he wanted confidential news of a relative. It was a dangerous thing to do, because once he gave the man Amparo's name, the man could harm him. He had no way of knowing whether the person at the other end of the wire was a fascist who might turn him in. But he received a friendly answer: 'I'm always at your disposal. You can count on my discretion because I would like to ask about someone in your zone.'

"So Emi said, 'Her name is Amparo Barayón, married to Ramón Sender.'

"And the other man answered, 'She's in jail but there are those who are trying to get her out.' Things remained like this for a long time. Every three or four days Emi asked after her whenever his shift coincided with his friend's at the other end. 'The baby has been taken to her in jail. Little is possible but there are those who have hope.' So that was how Emi learned that Amparo had been arrested, but he didn't tell me the worst had happened until much later."

Palmira: "Of course everyone hoped to survive, but basically Amparo was fearful. I remember her talking one day with my mother—we were seated on the floor—and she said, 'Yes, they're going to kill me.'

"'Come on, Amparo!' my mother said. 'Don't say that!'

"I have always remembered this conversation. She was a strong, intelligent woman, but she knew Ramón was writing in Madrid. She was afraid he would write something against Franco that would destroy her chances. But most of all, she felt her brother-in-law had led her into a trap."

If the military governor Claomarchirán dangled a passport as bait, it was a man named Viloria who killed Amparo for a reason, as we will ultimately learn, worse than any we could have imagined.

Pilar: "Segundo Viloria was a lawyer who represented the Conservative Party in Zamora. Everybody knew him and until then had considered him normal. However he was responsible for bringing in hundreds of women—it was his specialty. Among these unfortunate women was a certain Eugenia. He had beaten her so violently that when she entered our cell, her body was black and her underwear stuck to her wounds. After he beat her, he raped her, but he didn't stop there. When he was again on duty at the prison (as a member of the falange death squad), he once more sought out his victim and repeated his terrible acts. Some weeks passed, and then this monster came again one night to look for her. He led her to the cemetery and killed her there.

Palmira: "Viloria was a beast. He was paid to kill and he killed my father. He was one of a group of men who were paid to murder. They shot without knowing who their victims were. 'Kill this one,' the falangists would say. They would grab them and shoot twenty, thirty, forty, whomever they wanted. But he was not the one to denounce her. He shot her, but the person responsible for her death was he who denounced her. If there had not been denouncers, there would not have been assassins."

Pilar: "Another case of sadism worth mentioning is that of an assassin named Mariscal. He went freely about Zamora and committed so many terrible crimes that even his accomplices became afraid. Mariscal became one of the worst of the executioners because of the long succession of atrocities he perpetrated without regard to age, sex or the condition of the victims. These two murderers, Viloria and Mariscal, would have made an interesting study for psychiatrists."

Eugenia, Amparo's younger sister, hurried to Zamora when she heard of Amparo's arrest.

Eugenia: "When they decided to shoot Amparo, the military governor Claomarchirán told Sevilla to take charge of Andrea. 'I can't take the baby,' Sevilla said. Claomarchirán asked why. 'How could I face my wife with the baby in my arms and tell her that her sister was going to be killed that same night?' So they took Andrea to the orphanage."

Pilar: "Amparo Barayón, wife of the distinguished writer Ramón J. Sender . . . had with her in the cell her baby daughter Andrea. At six o'clock that evening, Justo, secretary to the administrator of the prison, dragged her child from her arms, saying, among other witticisms, that 'Reds did not have the right to nourish their children.'"

Palmira: "Justo snatched Andreina from her mother in the patio. Amparo tried to stop him but she couldn't. We were eating, and—. . . At this moment Amparo understood that she was going to be shot . . . The thing is that I don't remember much. These were moments of confusion. Moments that—you don't know what's happening—you're not trying to record these events. One doesn't think like this. They happen, and I have been told I have a trauma about this incident. Also, when someone was going to be shot, my mother protected me from the information. What happened was terrible."

Pilar: "Amparo, powerless to defend the baby, struggled and wept, a prey to indescribable madness. Then she wrote a farewell letter to Sender which I kept for a long time but had to tear into pieces and eat because of the continual searches to which we were subjected. In this letter she delivered her children to his care and held Miguel Sevilla for responsible for her death."

The text of Amparo's note:

> Beloved Ramón: Do not pardon my assassins who have
> robbed me of Andreina, nor Miguel Sevilla who is guilty

for having denounced me. For myself, I do not care because
I die for you. But what will become of the children? They
are yours now. I love you always, Amparo.

Pilar: "When she finished writing, Amparo fainted. When she
recovered, she remained in a state of semi-consciousness, crying for
her little girl."

From the article in INTERVIU magazine: "Hours before her assassination, Amparo was confessed by a priest . . . who explicitly
refused her absolution, alleging later in public that she had always
lived in sin because she had not been married by the Church . . . In
later confessions to the murder, Miguel Sevilla . . . said that 'Amparo's confession damaged her case very much.' One has to ask
whether the secret of confession was so devalued in those days, or
whether Sevilla only pretended to know to excuse himself for not
having moved a finger to save his sister-in-law . . .

"Minutes before midnight in the women's cell, the clattering of
Sra. Teresa's keys was heard. Shortly after the town clock struck
twelve . . . a harsh voice called the names of three women from the
lower level of the staircase: Amparo Barayón, Juliana Luís García
and her cousin Antonia Blanes Luís. When one of the women sum-
moned delayed in coming out, the voice shouted: 'Are you coming
down or do you want us to come up and get you?'

"The falangists in charge of the execution put them in a bus.
They were not handcuffed. Some minutes after midnight, the bus
left on the road to Salamanca en route to the cemetery."

Eugenia: "I believe Amparo left for the cemetery weeping and
shouting, 'My children, my children!'"

Zamora, 1981: The time had come to visit the cemetery, the moment of truth on my pilgrimage. I didn't feel ready for it, but it had
to be faced. We stopped to buy white gladiolas and red carnations at
a flower shop. Earlier that same day, my researcher Fernando had
told me that during the first few years after Amparo's death some
unknown person regularly had placed flowers on her grave.

South a few kilometers towards Salamanca, a high wall loomed
up on the left. The gate featured a statue of San Atilano, the patron
saint of the city. The graveyard contained rows of family tombs arranged between cypress trees. Amparo's final resting-place consisted

of a flat slab of ornate marble in front of a twelve-foot-high head-stone topped by a black cross. Below the cross, a thorn-crowned head of Christ was carved in high relief and below that, the words "Familia Ignacio Maes"—Magdalena's and Chori's father. It was by far the most ostentatious tomb in sight. On the elevated center slab, a plaque read:

AMPARO BARAYÓN MIGUEL

18-11-1936   Q.E.P. ("REST IN PEACE")

FROM HER HUSBAND RAMÓN J. SENDER

According to my sister's notes, the plaque was not added until after Franco's death because it was dangerous to do so. And the date was wrong, some obscure family mix-up at the time. The grave lay in full sun, the light reflected by the white stone blinding. She's in there, I kept thinking. I put the flowers in the receptacle below the agonized Christ. In my pocket I had a small box with the last bits of my father's bone and ash which I wanted to leave with Amparo.

"Oh no, we can't open the tomb!" Chori's husband exclaimed.

Chori pointed to a diamond-shaped ventilation hole in the front. "Would it fit in there?"

I measured the aperture. "Just barely."

She handed me a twig. "Push the box with this and it will fall inside." She explained how the interior consisted of a series of shelves, three on a side, and below them a bone pit, the ossuary. When the shelves were full, the first to have been interred was the first into the ossuary, a simple, practical system.

"So if I push the box far enough, it falls into the ossuary?" I asked.

"That's right."

Either I was going to make a production of this by insisting on an appointment to have the marble slab lifted, Amparo's casket opened and the ashes placed inside, or I was going to behave myself. I attached the box to the twig with the rubber band holding it shut and inserted it into the aperture. When I withdrew the twig, I heard the echo of its landing far below. It sounded very empty inside. Empty and far away. What should I do now?

How could such a beloved, endearing woman have been shot in the midst of her childhood paradise? Given what she remembered of Zamora, the logic of her decision to return was unassailable. "I'll go home where everybody loves me," she had decided. "Where I'll be safe." To have been betrayed by the relatives to whom she had returned for protection must have been the final disillusionment.

The heat was intense. I had never been so uncomfortable in my life. More than anything I wanted to claw open the tomb, lift the lid off the casket and take Amparo's poor bones to my breast. I wanted to wrest her out of the clutches of the three entities that had killed her, her family, her church and her town.

"Where was she originally buried?" I gasped. "Where did you find her?"

"They have completely redone the cemetery," the husband said. "It's not possible to see the spot."

I took photos to distract myself. If only I could have come out alone in a cab in the cool of the evening. And then what? I wanted to avoid people hanging around waiting for me to be through with something I hadn't even started. What utter frustration to have come across all these years, these thousands of miles, only to be stopped by a few feet of stone! But I had to understand, at last, that she was beyond my reach. I could never be next to her again. I had to acknowledge that my hunger to touch, to be with her, would never be satisfied.

On another day I returned to the cemetery, determined to spend the afternoon alone with Amparo. Seated beside her, I thought how the priest's refusal to give her final absolution must have brought her to the ultimate horror of her religion, a death without hope of redemption. According to the teachings she had professed throughout her early years, she would burn in hell for eternity.

Silently I offered up a prayer for Amparo. I did not pray to the Catholic Mary, nor to the Mary of the Crusades or the Inquisition, but to the Divine Mother of peace and gentleness who is offended by pomp and ceremony. Amparo left the church because it became unclean. If somehow she erred in this, I asked pardon for her.

Instead of the sign of the cross, that rack of pain upon which man's nature has been crucified by the priesthoods, I made the sign of the circle, placing Amparo within the shimmering blue sphere of Ariadne's childhood paradise.

Pacing up and down between the tombs, I wondered where Amparo could have drawn her last breath before Viloria pulled the trigger.

"Where did the fascists shoot them?" I asked several people.

"Against the far wall," an elderly couple told me.

"Beside the tall stone cross beside the entrance," two mainte-nance men replied.

I closed my eyes and allowed my intuition to lead me to . . . a spot on a side path which inexplicably attracted me. It might have been here, on a cold October night, that Amparo finally crossed the frontiers of Spain, but not into Portugal or France.

CHAPTER 12: **EUGENIA'S VISIT AND UNCLE MANOLO'S EXECUTION**

Two hours north of Zamora in the cathedral town of Astorga, I met with Amparo's younger sister Eugenia and her husband Delfín, a retired civil guard. They remembered the tragic aftermath and added even worse details.

Eugenia: "When I arrived in Zamora on October tenth, I went first to the café. Casimira phoned me there to invite me to spend the night. I wanted to go to the jail to visit Amparo right away, but Sevilla said, 'Don't go.' He already knew they were going to kill her that night. 'They'll argue with you about a safe conduct pass from the governor. You can't just go at any hour.' And the next morning, he no more than left the house when he came back and told me Amparo had been shot."

Suddenly the room in which we sat listening to these horrors filled with a chorus of rasping shrieks, like fingernails clawing slate. The swallows nesting outside the window were just settling down for the night, but it sounded like some mythical creature beating its wings against the walls. Everyone fell silent, waiting for the avenging angel to pass. It was *lubricán*, the twilight hour when, according to my father, men in Aragon turned into wolves and murdered their loved ones.

I tried to regain my composure by asking the next question on my notepad. "And the date for Antonio's death?"

"We knew nothing!" Eugenia protested. "I was living in León and my husband had been ordered to his barracks!"

I was surprised by the sudden vociferousness of her response. Obviously she was replying more to some inner voice than to me. Had she also felt that instant of horror?

"In those moments there was nothing we could do!" her husband sputtered. "I was a civil guard and had to be where I was posted. I couldn't even accompany Eugenia on her trip to Zamora. Also, I did not know Amparo, but they judged everyone in the family the same." He was speaking as if I had accused him for not having rushed to Amparo's assistance. "I thought this way: 'I should go beg for my in-laws' lives, but the falangists will start believing that . . . and I have two infant children!'" He paused, frowning to himself. "These were moments you cannot understand unless you lived through them. The Civil War was a despicable thing. They took people away for nothing!" His voice subsided into mutters behind the general conversation.

"We have Amparo's radio put away," a cousin told me. "Would you like to see it?" He brought out a large box tied with twine.

I hefted it. Heavy! How had Amparo managed to carry it all the way from San Rafael? I unpacked it and stared at it in awe, a Phillips in a wooden case. The dial had yellowed. The tubes were the size of pint bottles. At last something from her past! Amparo's fingers had touched these knobs, and no doubt mine also. How many long hours had she spent beside it, her head bowed beside the speaker to listen to forbidden broadcasts from Radio Madrid?

"Take it with you," Eugenia offered.

"Perhaps just the case and speaker," I replied. "The radio probably won't run on American current anyway."

On the way to the station for our return to Madrid, Eugenia mentioned another grotesque detail: "Two years after Amparo's death, the news spread that Franco was going to visit Zamora. He wanted to find out who was responsible for all the murders. The falangists decided to cover their tracks and appear innocent, so they brought in Casimira and Magdalena. They forced them to sign a certificate stating that Amparo had died of pneumonia."

Our train stopped at Medina del Campo, where Amparo was first arrested. Red-bricked Castle de la Mota glowered over the landscape as if daring someone to beseige it. Queen Juana la Loca holed up here after travelling all of Castile with the corpse of her husband King Philip I. When my spirits were low, I could identify with her because I was crisscrossing Spain carrying an unavenged and unshriven mother in my heart. According to Amparo's understanding of the tenets of her religion, the best she could have hoped for was to enter Purgatory. Or perhaps she remained earthbound because of her concern for her children. My sister once told me how, as a three-year-old, she had awakened at daybreak one morning to see the dark silhouette of a woman pacing the floor at the foot of her bed. She always believed it was Amparo who had visited her.

At my cousin Ana María's, Conchita welcomed us home. "Oh! I have something for you! Here! Here!" She handed me a photo. "It's the only one like it in the whole world." She stared over my shoulder. "She was prettier than that. She had a lovely figure and she was tall."

I was looking at a picture of my father and Amparo. Never before had I seen one of them together. He looked very natty in a full-length double-breasted leather overcoat and gloves, Amparo in a rakish hat and black coat. She was taller than he by perhaps two inches, although she might have been wearing heels. He looked every bit the successful young journalist, while she had a stoop-shouldered, delicate air about her. Incredible how different she seemed in every photo! Perhaps her hair was the reason, because here she was wearing it shorter than elsewhere.

Conchita described how she and Emi had been transferred to Burgos, the capital of the rebel zone, a month or so after Amparo left for Zamora. "All this time I thought my brother Manolo was in France with Marcelle and her family. They were supposed to have gone there in early July on vacation with her parents. Anyway, a delegation arrived from Huesca to Burgos and I was eager for news." She smoothed the wrinkles of her dress. "You have to remember that all communications had been stopped, even telephone conversations and telegrams. So this commercial delegation arrived from Huesca to ask for help because the town was being besieged by republican forces. They knew Emi had been transferred to Burgos and phoned him at work.

"'Well, Emi, we're here for twenty-four hours!' they said. 'Let's meet at one of the Plaza Mayor bars before lunch.'

"Emi agreed and phoned me to join him. 'Perhaps they'll have news!'

"They were all acquaintances of ours, so I went down around two o'clock. 'Well, Santa María,' I said to one of them. 'Any word about Manolo? He's in France, right?'

"'You don't know about Manolo?' he asked in amazement.

"'What?' I said in growing alarm. 'What has happened?'

She slapped her thigh. "'They shot him in Huesca on the thirteenth of August!'"

"Right there, in the middle of the plaza with all the bars filled, I began to scream! 'Assassins! Scum! You're all a band of scoundrels from Franco right on down to the bottom!' I had kept quiet for so long, so quiet, making excuses for what was happening.

"The others began pleading with me, 'Conchita, por Díos! Conchita!' Emi was signaling desperately for a taxi. He found one and put me in it. One of them reentered the bar and said, 'Look, she suffers from nervous attacks. She can't control what she says—sometimes she even says she's a saint!'

"Emi said, 'They'll never leave Burgos because we're all going to jail!'

"In the taxi, poor Santa María said to Emi, 'If you had warned me I wouldn't have told her!'

"When we got back to the house, I was still acting like a crazy woman. 'We must get away!' I was screaming. 'These people are all assassins! We have to leave this zone! I'll live anywhere else, even in an open field! We're living among killers!' I couldn't stop!" She sighed. "That's how I learned about my brother."

"Poor Emi said to me, 'Don't you realize you're endangering everyone? They can have us all shot!'

"This is why Emi told me only much later in Zaragoza of how he learned of Amparo's death from the telegrapher in Zamora. He said to me, 'How could I have told you about Amparo? If I had told you then . . .'"

From family members including Manolo's widow Marcelle I learned details of Manolo's arrest and murder. On the night the Civil War began, he worked late at his office.

Marcelle phoned her sister-in-law. "Listen, we haven't left on vacation because Manolo has so much work," she said. "Let's come have supper at your house."

When they arrived, everyone talked of going to the movies, because in Huesca they only had movies on Saturday. But that night Manolo remained glued to the radio in amazement. The announcer was reporting the uprisings in all the cities. Suddenly all over Spain everyone was in the streets with weapons.

"Come to the table!" Marcelle called to him. "We're eating!"

"Let me be," he replied. "Things are very bad."

When the news was over, he asked Marcelle to go directly home with him.

"Aren't we going to the movies?" she asked.

"This isn't a night for the movies or anything else," he replied.

When they left, the town was in an uproar, the workers and the fascists threatening to kill each other, firing shots in the streets. He stayed at home quietly for a few days. Then the police came looking for him. Since they were all friends of his, they encouraged him to escape.

"Manolo, you'd better leave the country. Do you have a passport?"

"If I go, it will look like I'm running away," he replied. "I've done nothing wrong. I don't have to hide myself." He was very noble. "I don't have to escape because no one can harm me. Go ahead and do your duty."

They arrested him and put him in the guardhouse of the jail. There, on the thirteenth of August, without a trial or any formal accusation, he was taken to the cemetery and shot along with three others. The bodies were dumped together in a common grave.

Marcelle: "Manolo's assassins were four men. One was from Canfranc where I lived, where my father was Director of Customs. His family had a bakery and every day he brought our bread. I knew him by sight. But he was a fascist and they paid him. Don't believe they were volunteers. They were paid killers. He told someone, 'I hunt wild goats in the mountains. I'm a good shot. Assure the lady whom I have seen so often that Manolo did not suffer. I killed him with one bullet.'" With a tapered index finger she pointed to her head. It entered here and exited behind. It wasn't necessary to give him the *coup de grace*. The night they shot him I was awake. I heard the cars leaving the jail. I thought, 'They are going to kill someone.'

They were already killing many people. At three in the morning I heard shots. It's because of this that I still awaken many times at this hour."

We arrived in Huesca on the thirteenth of August, the forty-sixth anniversary of Uncle Manolo's assassination. Our visit coincided with The Feast of San Lorenzo, the town's patron saint, a week-long event that brought thousands of visitors. A hotel room was out of the question, so we had phoned my Aunt Carmen, my father's youngest sister, at her summer place in Jaca. She and her husband would be glad to pick us up at the Huesca bus depot. They drove us to the cemetery through festive crowds of young people wearing the traditional green caps and neckerchiefs of the saint. I wanted to spill the drops of Papá's blood which Benedicta had washed out of his bedroom carpet beside Uncle Manolo. It would be a symbolic reunion with the brother he loved so much.

From *Counterattack in Spain,* I remembered my father's eulogy to a fallen comrade. The soldier had fallen forward on his face and in his death agony his fingernails had scraped the loose earth into small mounds. His open eyes stared at the soil of Spain, as if to memorize the precious substance he was dying to protect. There was a passionate frenzy in his expression as if he was clutching his beloved to him in an outpouring of love.

My father thought, 'Our dead are not repugnant to me. Go, comrade, take with you that precious earth which you grasp. It's yours, now and forever. The land is yours by a divine right greater than that of kings, than that of Franco's filthy, vulgar pretenders. All they have done is mortgage your soil to the German and Italian generals. But their own lies will condemn them and the land will be ours. Enriched by our blood, the calcium of our bones, it will nourish another strong generation in whose songs you will live, in whose lives you will be remembered.'

Before our departure for Málaga and Barcelona we paid a final visit to Conchita in Madrid. Standing by the elevator, I took her hand. "Best of all on this journey has been meeting you," I told her.

"If only you knew how long I waited to see you again! How many times I wondered how you and your sister were. When your father returned to France in 1962, the whole family went to visit him in Pau and I said to him, 'You must put me in contact with the children.' And he said, 'No! Because I know how you are and you'll tell them the truth of the tragedy of their mother. I don't want them to know! Perhaps when they're old, but I don't want their childhood, their youth, to be embittered.'" She stared up at me with great tenderness. "You cannot know what a mother you had in Amparo. She did not die just once, but three or four times. She was such a mother! For her, the most horrible was to think of her children uncared for,—*desamparados*—abandoned."

A

s the train pulled into Málaga, my anticipation built. At last we would meet Amparo's niece Magdalena, the person who had kept her memory most alive. Her testimony, delivered with quiet authority, would resolve many of the conflicting details I had heard from others. Would Magdalena meet us? I didn't even know what she looked like.

"*Hola*, Ramón?" A thin woman with her gray hair done up in a topknot approached us. She had a long, intelligent face.

Beside her stood her husband, a bushy-browed, professorial type with a briar pipe in his mouth. He drove us through downtown, pointing out the harbor and lighthouse, the flourishing park across from the two ancient fortresses the Alcazaba and Gibralfaro which had protected the coastline in olden days.

Their apartment, two blocks from the beach, was lined with books. One bookcase contained the most complete collection of my father's I had ever seen.

Over *aperitifs*, Magdalena kept glancing at me with a bow-shaped smile on her lips. I thought of the tensions fostered by my father in our relationship. God only knew what he had told her. In his San Diego apartment I had found her correspondence reporting my requests for information and including photocopies of my letters. Now that he had died, I hoped she would prove as loyal to me.

"Eugenia said Amparo was arrested after insulting the military governor." I told her.

"This much is certain," Magdalena replied. "The police came to the house and arrested her. I know because I went to the apartment every day to see you. One morning when I arrived, the servant girl said, 'No, she isn't here. They took her away.'

"I told my mother. That afternoon they transferred Amparo from the police station to the jail. But when they told her they were taking her to prison, she tried to escape. She was fearful of leaving you and Andreina. But when she started to run, she tripped and fell in front of the post office."

But where could she have run? Where in such a small town could she have hidden with two children? Despair had overwhelmed her, and she had responded like a hunted deer.

"Who visited Amparo in jail?" I asked.

"My father, and Aisia many times. My mother, Eugenia and Nati did all they could to help her. You see, Amparo was arrested twice in Zamora," Magdalena continued in her subdued manner. "The first time she told them who she was and that she wanted to go to Portugal. But it wasn't possible—the frontier had been closed—and they let her go because she hadn't committed any offense. The second time, someone in the family denounced her."

"Miguel Sevilla."

"Miguel Sevilla was against everyone," Magdalena admitted. "The family was very divided. Sevilla was not one of us. I believe he was very guilty for Amparo's death. Very guilty. Because he knew all about the killings ahead of time." Her mouth tightened into a thin line. "It's very sad to have to say this to you."

"So Sevilla was the one."

"Something like that," Magdalena replied. "My mother kept saying he would save Amparo, that he would do what was possible. Also, Casimira could have done something. She was the French teacher for Claomarchirán's children. My mother said to her, 'Please, let's go talk with him.' As military governor he was the one who signed the releases for those in prison. He gave people permission to leave and then they would be taken to the cemetery and killed." She gestured helplessly. "But Casimira said no and explained that the governor had been informed and would not permit anything to happen to Amparo. She wouldn't be released to the death squads. Why was Casimira like this? Because she thought if Amparo was put out of the way, she and Sevilla would get more of the family money." She shook her head sorrowfully. "It's horrible to have to admit that a family member could do such a thing. But I was present in the café the night Miguel Sevilla came in and said, 'Tonight they are killing Amparo.'

Shocked and incredulous, I leaned forward. "He said this to whom?"

"To everyone." She hesitated. "I was overcome with emotion. Casimira and Sevilla came to the café because we were taking inventory. The court had seized everything as war goods. We were holding a family council, and they had an interest in the property, although it was in the names of the uncles. They said to my mother, 'Tonight they are killing Amparo.' And my mother couldn't do anything. It was horrible! Between the two of them, Casmira and Sevilla could have saved her."

Perhaps Sevilla, head of the local *requeté* militia and with close connections to the church, could have interceded for Amparo, something he was unlikely to do after having denounced her. And Casimira, with her easy entré into the Claumarchirán family, might have wielded some influence. But I believe the truth lay closer to what Palmira Sanjuan said: Amparo was given up for lost by her family after her arrest, and the surviving members distanced themselves from her. Magdalena's parents were paralyzed with fear along with the majority of the citizens of Zamora. Her father expected daily to be arrested himself.

Later I mentioned how I had heard two versions of where I lived while Amparo was in jail, with Amparo's elderly aunt Maximina and in the orphanage.

"Both are true," Magdalena said. "Maximina took you first, and then after Amparo was killed you were taken to the orphanage at the governor's order. My mother went every day to bring you things and see how you were. The nuns were very kind. Then when Dr. Junod came, the director of the Red Cross's Spanish relief effort, they arranged for an ambulance to take you and Andrea to France.

"When Dr. Junod asked, 'Why was Amparo killed?', they answered him, 'It was a mistake. An error.'"

"She was killed by mistake?" I repeated, stunned.

"An error. We had then a type of open proceedings called 'political responsibilities.' My mother was called to appear, and since this Red Cross man had come to search for you, they called for Amparo also. They cited Amparo as if she were alive! They sent a subpoena as if she weren't dead and said to my mother, 'Why doesn't this Amparo present herself with you others?'

"'I don't know,' my mother lied. 'They took her from the house one day and we don't know anything else.'

"It was necessary to pretend ignorance because there were those who would have shot my mother also." Magdalena paused. "I remember seeing you and your sister leave together with Dr. Junod, Tía Maximina, Andrea's wetnurse and a Swiss count. Also, Sevilla went with you."

"What? Sevilla?"

"You didn't know that?" Magdalena asked.

What unbelievable gall the man had! To denounce Amparo and then accompany us to the frontier!

"But why?" I exclaimed. "That's the most bizarre thing I have heard!"

"He did it to prove he was kind," Magdalena admitted.

She went on to describe how, when Antonio was shot, no one knew where his body was. "My mother went with Casimira in a taxi to visit Saturnino in the Toro jail. When they had gone halfway, they were stopped by a falangist with a rifle. 'Could you take me with you?' he asked. Clearly they couldn't say no. So he got in. 'I come from burying some pigs which the dogs dug up,' he said." Her face stiffened in anguish. "My mother had to listen with all the pain of knowing they had killed her brother. When they arrived at the jail, the warden said, 'Please, don't enter dressed in black! No! And don't tell Saturnino his brother is dead! Say he's in another jail, because there are falangists here who will arrest you too.'

"The warden was a good man and took them to his wife who gave them normal clothing to wear. They put it on and went to visit their brother, but there was a falangist listening to everything that was said. When Saturnino asked, 'Where is Antonio?', they had to answer, 'Don't worry, he's all right. He's in the Fermoselles jail.'" Her mouth drooped. "Later they shot Saturnino along with thirty-six others in reprisal for a civil guard's son who was killed at the front—near where you were in San Rafael. When the father heard the news of his son's death, he went to the Toro jail and began saying, 'This one, this one, this one!' without knowing who they were. Thirty-six were shot, among them my uncle and many of my uncle's acquaintances."

The conversation shifted to the priest who denied Amparo absolution.

"He was a young man because now he's over eighty," Magdalena said. "He lives in a residence somewhere. On the day after they killed Amparo, my mother went to find where they had buried her. Since she had already lost both brothers and had not been able to recover their bodies, she was very distressed. She was weeping by the pole where they shot their victims and there to one side was the grave."

"A pole in the cemetery?" I repeated.

"They put a light on top of a tall pole in the middle of the cemetery to shoot by, and there they killed people. They buried Amparo next to the light, which they did many times. There was a mound of earth of the sort they put over one and that's where she was. There was no marker—nothing. My mother ordered that a cross be placed there." Magdalena paused. "My mother was there crying and this same priest came by. 'Are you related to Amparo?' he asked.

" 'I am her sister,' she said.

" 'I heard her confession,' he said. 'I definitely did not give her absolution.'

"This was what that priest said—to my mother! And she asked him why.

" 'Because she was not married by the Church,' he replied.

Her voice trailed off. "It was I who went some years later to recover the body. My paternal grandfather had died. He was in his final illness when the tomb was being built, but he died before it was finished. When they gave us permission to move his body into the tomb, we also asked permission to move Amparo. The same day we disinterred them both. My mother said, 'You dig up Amparo's remains.' I was seventeen years old." She paused, her face suddenly gaunt. "The bad thing was they put quicklime in with her. There was no coffin or anything, just the body and quicklime."

I pondered the image of a seventeen-year-old girl forced to recover the remains of her favorite aunt. She had to brush the dirt off the bones and gather them together, to perform the ritual every part of me yearned to have accomplished. All at considerable danger to herself. Perhaps that was one reason she was jailed five years later.

I mentioned how in Zamora we met the son of the military governor in the Civil Registry and questioned him at his apartment.

"I knew the elder Claomarchirán," her husband muttered around his pipe. "He was a man inflated by his authority. As military governor he had all the power in the world to stop the killings but he was a weak man."

"He signed the exit papers which allowed the death squads to take their victims," Magdalena said. "But not the death orders. He authorized their leaving prison but did not know where they went." She placed her hands in her lap. "I imagine he did know, but he didn't sign for their deaths."

"Those who provoked this catastrophe were very few," her husband added. "Very few from one side and very few from the other."

"The Right did much more than the others," Magdalena said. "The coup attempt on the twenty-third of February—"

"However!" Her husband used the word to slice through her response. "People died on one side and died on the other. But the majority—they were horrified! They had to continue living together. Today, if you were to ask in Zamora who the guilty ones were, there were only six, seven, or nine men. No more!"

"True," Magdalena agreed. "There weren't more. It was just that one half of the city confronted the other half."

"Who were the killers?" I asked.

"The one who shot Amparo was a lawyer," Magdalena replied. "Segundo Viloria."

Magdalena nodded. "Viloria. He courted Amparo at one time. He fell in love with her. But Amparo told him, 'No!'"

I gasped in amazement. "What?"

"That's what happened," her husband concurred. "That's history."

What a grotesque twist! Viloria was doing more than following orders. He was avenging himself on the woman who had resisted his advances. Unbelievable!

Magdalena gave a quirky smile. "One day I looked out the window and saw Viloria on the street below, talking with some men—I must have been twelve or thirteen. I took a flowerpot and dropped it!" Her eyes twinkled with amusement. "The pot missed him, but it was a big one and shattered. He looked up and saw me. My mother said, 'But child, they'll come and kill us all! They know who lives here!'"

Her husband relit his pipe. "I returned to Zamora in 1937 and

Viloria was hated throughout the city. He had passed his lawyer's exams, but he did not work. People would not bring him their business—nothing at all. He was totally repudiated and rejected by everyone."

"The other part of the guilt for Amparo's death must be Ramón's—a disagreeable thing but true," Magdalena said. "He should never have told her to return to Zamora."

I nodded. "And I have been told Amparo was afraid he would write something for the Madrid papers that would seal her fate. Did many people know Amparo was the wife of Ramón Sender?"

"Yes, everyone knew. It was a small town and your father was very well known. I read his books when I was young, even before the war. The bookstores carried them."

"If Amparo knew that people in Zamora knew she was Ramón's wife, why did she return?"

"Because she didn't think there would be trouble. Zamora had always been so peaceful."

"When she arrived and found Saturnino and Antonio in jail, why didn't she try to escape?"

"How? There were no possibilities. You needed a safe conduct pass to go anywhere. To go to the university in Salamanca for my exams, I needed a paper like a passport. And that was many years later." She got to her feet. "I have copies for you of the letters Amparo wrote to Aisia." She crossed to the desk and handed me some pages.

The letters at last! These were the first words of my mother I had seen since I lost that typewritten copy of her farewell note as a teenager—and the first time I had ever seen her handwriting. The first letter was dated September 9, 1936:

> Dear Aisia:
> I have so many things to tell you but they are only moments of anguish. I enclose a letter for Ramón's grandfather. Address: José Sender, Huesca. I don't remember the street. Put on the letter, 'If you can't find him, please forward to Joaquín Monrás at the wine shop.' Joaquín is my sister-in-law's husband. Regarding the children, I would like you to have everything you need until you can return them to their father. With or without me, don't separate yourself from them. At best you all may be able to return

before me to Madrid, depending on the freedom (to move about). Other food—please observe: in the morning some Neave cereal, at midday after three and one-half hours a broth of vegetables or a bouillon without fat, the rest of the milk and then another portion of Neave. If he has more appetite, milk, but I think this is enough. To one spoonful of Neave add two of sugar.

Don't forget to tell Ramón that I love him very much. Kiss Monchín and don't forget that I love you with all my soul. Write to my brothers . . . Many kisses to all.
Amparo

The second letter is undated but obviously written later because of its context:

Dear Aisia:

I received your letter for which I thank you with all my soul. I don't think you're telling me the truth because you ask for the address of Ramón's father. The address in Huesca I don't remember, as you know,—I have quite a bad memory. Miss Maruja's address is in a suburb of Madrid—I believe it is Canillejas. Doubtless they have been at her mother-in-law's house for a month and there she'll give birth. Moreover, since he is a lieutenant in the artillery, he isn't going to leave her alone in the house. As far as Huesca is concerned, because Don José Sender is a lawyer and well known, it isn't difficult to find him, if he is alive. You know what it must mean to have one son on each side when you are seventy years old. Write me often and tell me everything. Baby Andreina yesterday was peevish. I'm sending you a letter that you must carry in a sealed envelope to Don José María Cid who lives next door to the Barayón house. Kisses to everyone, with my heart for my son Ramón,
Amparo

Amparo's letters were treasures, making her more real to me than even her photographs. Her instructions regarding my diet, written after weeks of nightmarish confinement, displayed her motherly concern for me even more than her messages of love.

In her desperation she had been trying to contact anyone who could help her because she mentioned people to whom Aisia was to forward notes. Why to my Aunt Maruja? Probably to find out where my father was or to let him know what was happening. Why did she ask Aisia to write "my brothers" if one was dead and the other imprisoned? She must have meant her brothers-in-law. Her concern for my grandfather Don José whose sons were fighting on different sides demonstrated her compassion for others in the midst of the hell in which she had been trapped.

The writing was hurried, distracted, the words hard to read. The last paragraph of the first letter was finished in pencil, as if her pen went dry. The originals either had been destroyed by my father or, more likely, remained in the hands of his compulsive archivist Margareta. Why hadn't I received these letters years ago? What a difference it would have made to have read my mother's caring words!

"Do you think my parents had a happy marriage?" I asked Magdalena.

"I doubt if Amparo and Ramon's relationship would have lasted," she replied. "Personally, I don't think they were even married."

What an ironic twist! Did Amparo suffer months of anguish for a husband who would have ultimately abandoned her? As far as their having been married, Conchita's description of the wedding contradicted Magdalena's statement.

"Your father had a woman friend in Madrid during the summer and fall of 1936," she said quietly. "I was with him when he was signing books at the Book Fair in Madrid in 1974. This woman gave him a kiss and said she was his girlfriend during the War. I wasn't able to find out who she was."

So my father had been unfaithful while Amparo was in jail. All those months while Amparo had been sleeping on the floor of a crowded cell, he had been leading the life of a carefree bachelor in Madrid. And writing his important communiqués from the front, any one of which could have sealed her fate if they had fallen into fascist hands. Even if I acknowledged his need for a sexual outlet as natural, the image left a bitter taste in my mouth.

Later, Magdalena handed me a wrapped parcel which contained a large full-face portrait photo of Amparo in an oval, gilded frame. This was her special present to me and was the best photo of all because it delineated Amparo's features in detail, the indentation between the mouth and nose which I had inherited, the same upper lip and chin. I judged her to be in her mid-twenties. Although her nose was too Roman to type her as a classic beauty, her eyes were large and expressive.

On a visit to friends, I played some Chopin nocturnes on the piano while everyone sat in the patio arbor. I chose them especially for Magdalena because I was sure she had heard Amparo play them. It was my way of telling her that Amparo lived on in her son. I tried to give the phrases the same shading and lilt that I imagined Amparo might have given them.

When the time came, it was hard to say goodbye. Our few days together had put to rest much accumulated misunderstanding. The moment Magdalena and I met, our distrust had dissolved because we sought and found in each other aspects of the woman we both loved.

In Barcelona we visited Asunción, the tiniest, brightest (according to all family opinions) and feistiest of my Sender aunts. A red-haired, elegantly coiffed lady, she stood with the same military thrust-back shoulders of Papá and Conchita. From the way she kept throwing emotion-packed glances at me, it seemed my visit was of extreme importance to her.

"I lost everything under Franco," she stated. "They took away my degrees, my right to work. I had to teach in Switzerland because no Spanish college would give me a job. I was in prison for a year and a half. A year and a half! I have nothing from before the War—no photos, no belongings." She stared at me with that peculiar intensity I had noticed earlier. "Come with me into the other room, Ramón. I have something I must tell you."

She was dead serious. What secret could not be bared before her husband and my wife? Seated in the hallway beside me, she continued. "Many times I was on the verge of telling this to your father, but I could not bring myself to." She fell silent, frowning. "Now he has died without my having done so, but I want you to know." She drew a deep breath and leaned closer. "I was in jail a year and a half in Zaragoza and San Sebastián. They transferred me to San Sebastián with my son who was just a baby at the time. I entered prison hand-cuffed to some civil guards." She inhaled deeply and sighed. "I stayed in the San Sebastián jail for eight months and in these jails you eventually hear everything. If you stay a day or a week, you learn nothing. But when you're in there a long time, you hear all the

Amparo Barayón, approximately twenty-two years old (1926). Folds in the original photograph suggest it had been rolled up and hidden for numerous years before being framed.

The Maes/Barayón family in Zamora, circa 1963. Cousin Magdalena ("Nena") is third from left, second row. Mother Magdalena (Amparo's half-sister) is second from right, second row. Magdalena's husband Timoteo (with mustache) is third row center.

news. In that jail, there was a Basque woman who had been in prison with your mother. She told me a detail that I have not heard anywhere else. I don't know if it's the truth, but it seems to me that you have the right to know."

She had me hanging on her words in suspense. Come on, out with it! I screamed inwardly. But if anything, the closer she approached her topic, the slower her words.

"She told me that . . . on your mother . . . they used . . . psychic torture.'

"Psychic torture?" I repeated in stupefaction.

"And that she died insane." She pierced me with a glance. "Can you bear to hear this?"

"Huh," I grunted, as if punched in the diaphragm. Her disclosure, horrifying as it was, only verified what I had already sensed. "What do you mean by 'psychic torture?'" I asked.

"Brainwashing," she replied. "And she died insane." She grasped my shoulder. "Your father suffered such guilt, and yet I always felt he had a right to know. But when I arrived at the moment of telling him, I didn't dare. You are younger and stronger . . ."

"I always believed the worst," I muttered half to myself. "I believed she was raped and tortured physically."

"Physical torture, no."

"But then what?"

"The type the Gestapo used in the concentration camps. They dedicated themselves during Amparo's last days to torturing her psychically, saying things such as that she was jailed because of your father, that he had denounced her, telling her horrors she could not possibly understand until finally she lost her reason." She paused to allow the image of my mother, crazed and out of control, to burn into my mind. "I just couldn't say this to Pepe because he was always so dejected when he spoke of Amparo."

"So psychic torture consisted of—"

"Speaking badly of the family and presenting lies as if they were the truth, just to make one suffer. Telling horrible things, gossip, as if they were poetry."

"According to Pilar's testimony, the jailer in Zamora was terrible," I replied. "They called her 'the Hyena' and she always taunted the married women by telling them their husbands were sleeping with other women or by describing the death agonies of those they shot."

Asunción nods. "The same in Zaragoza and San Sebastián. If one was bad, the other was worse. These are things one wants to forget, but they form the course of one's life." She leaned against the wall, her eyes half closed. "They also used psychic torture on me regarding your father. This I could never tell him. They took me into a room and said, 'Your brother is killing, he's raping nuns . . .' I knew nothing, but I knew what they were insinuating. With me the torture wasn't so deep, so strong. I could deal with it. But with Amparo, because they were thinking of killing her, they forced it more."

According to Asunción, psychic torture consisted of taunting and verbal bullying rather than sleep deprivation, bright lights, solitary confinement or other refinements. Of course the Spanish Inquisition had included all these subtler forms of pressure among their gruesome repertoire. No doubt the Civil War refined these brutal techniques. The terrible irony in Amparo's case was that, when she was told her husband was sleeping with other women, it was unfortunately true. Pilar had described how the nuns also harangued the women: 'You have sinned against the Holy Spirit, you are damned forever, your soul will be in torment.' Their accusations were designed to wrest a full confession and a change of heart. But the worst suffering for Amparo must have been her deep worry and concern for her children and her husband. To be told he was dead or had abandoned her must have pierced her like a knife.

I could see where after weeks of imprisonment, from within that vacuum of total isolation, the repetition of such brutal remarks could have brought Amparo to the breaking point. She was a woman of high-strung temperament. I could only hope that when she finally lost control, she had told her torturers exactly what filth they were.

"They also were going to kill me," Asunción admitted. "They pushed me along the corridor with rifles in my back. 'Let's finish her off!' they kept shouting. But they didn't do it because they hadn't been given the order. They were only amusing themselves a little at my expense. You have no idea how terrible it was inside those walls! We would hear screams when the death sentence was read to the prisoners."

"My hope is that Amparo lost consciousness during those last hours," I said. "The body has its own anesthesia." I paused because Asunción's words had brought me to the cutting edge of rage and grief.

When I could speak, I said, "I always have been caught between two impulses—vengeance and forgiveness. In Zamora I felt at times a terrible thirst for revenge, but at the same time I thought how important it is for Spain to forget what happened and start afresh."

Asunción gave a fierce snort. "Now listen to me! Those rightist beasts are the ones who injure others, while those of the left are always asked to pardon the injuries done to them. The rightists always inflict pain for no good reason and we, who have suffered so much, have to forgive and forget! They, in the meanwhile, without the remotest cause, <u>nothing</u>, pick up their weapons and go out on the sidewalk to shut down democracy!" She sat bolt upright. "And today it's just the same! Right now! On February 23rd, 1981, when the *Cortes* were invaded, my husband Daniel and I were here in this house and he said, 'Now it begins again,' and in this we were in agreement. Daniel also was condemned to six years." Her lips tightened. "The killings didn't stop when the war ended. Even on September 25th 1975, just before Franco finally died, the government shot five political prisoners."

CHAPTER 14

MY FATHER FROM
JULY 1936 TO
APRIL 1939

AND what about my father? In *Counter-attack In Spain*, published in the middle of the Civil War, he described how he and the Riveras crossed the mountain safely on that hot July day when they escaped from San Rafael. In Guadarrama, the Riveras caught a ride to Madrid. Ramón volunteered for the militia and spent the next days with a rifle slowing the rebels' advance towards the capital. Then he returned to the offices of *La Libertad* and wrote up his experiences. He enrolled in the Fifth Regiment and returned to a Guadarrama half destroyed by enemy artillery. His life fell into a rhythm: time at the front and then Madrid to write articles. After spending one sleepless night at the apartment haunted by memories of Amparo and the children, he took a room in the mansion that had been assigned to the Cultura Popular team. Occasionally he travelled with them to battle zones where they distributed pamphlets and periodicals.

In August, his patrol was assigned to an artillery battery at *Cabeza Lijar* near Peguerinos. Through his binoculars, he could see *Villa Frutos* in San Rafael below him. He adjusted the focus and caught a hint of movement in the lane. Soldiers. It was impossible that Amparo was still there. She must have taken his advice and returned to the safety of her family in Zamora. A few days later, fascist bombers decimated the battery and they had to move the guns by hand under cover of darkness. Back in Madrid for the funeral of the Peguerinos commanding officer, he met a woman soliciting donations of bed linen for military hospitals. Before the afternoon was over, they had slept together. She or someone like her became his lover over the next months. His patrol elected him captain and they were transferred to the Tagus River lines. There he rose in rank to major (*Comandante*).

In early October, Franco boasted of taking Madrid by October 12th, but the day came and went without any important victory. The roads to Madrid were choked with refugees. They camped in the subway stations while thousands of men dug trenches on the outskirts. Morale among the troops remained high in spite of rumors that the government was preparing to flee to Valencia.

The Luftwaffe bombers came over daily. They were painted white, the traditional color worn at children's funerals, and seemed to prefer to drop their loads on the narrow streets of the workers' suburbs. Militiamen shouted for everyone to take cover in the nearest cellars. Often that was not protection enough, because frequently a two-hundred-pound bomb smashed through the upper floors before exploding in the basement.

On the morning they bombed *La Cuesta de Santo Domingo*, thirteen children were among the thirty killed. On a little street close to the *Cava Baja*, a bomb fell on a line of women waiting to buy milk. Eleven died, one with a baby in her arms. Never before in war had a civilian population been so vulnerable to violent death because never before had airplanes been used for such gruesome purposes. Sometimes the bombs dropped on a 'school group,' the little shelters in gardens, and seventy, eighty—in one instance three hundred and nine children were killed. In this last case, the whole city was thrown into mourning. Why the children? Why tear life away from five and six-year-olds? The only explanation was that Franco and his generals hoped to exploit terror in the same way Hitler and Himmler used it, and they made the same miscalculation. Dying Spanish mothers called out to their sons, "Grow up quickly and learn to shoot a rifle before the Beast devours everything!"

Ramón witnessed scene after scene of desolation. He saw a militiaman weeping over the ruins of his home. The man had returned on a three-day furlough to find his wife, his children and parents all dead. "Those tears will create a barrier against which the fascists will find no successful weapon," Ramón wrote. "They give a tone to the heart and a strength to the muscle which become an insuperable obstacle to the science of the modern army."

At the end of October, Russian tanks, planes and officers arrived in Madrid. In return, the Bank of Spain's gold was sent to Russia under tight security. What other country could the Republic trust with the coin and bullion bars? Valued at 500 million dollars, it acted as collateral for the purchase of arms, oil and other necessities. Stalin threw a banquet to celebrate its arrival at which he said, "The Spaniards will never see their gold again, just as one cannot see one's own ears!"

Ramón's company, transformed into a battalion, received orders to become part of a brigade going to Valdemoros south of Madrid. He had been appointed Chief of Staff under the communist general Lister, a quarryman who had risen rapidly through the ranks. In spite of Lister's heroism and intelligence, the wheel of fate had handed him a series of defeats. Although Ramón professed great admiration for Lister, he was not altogether happy with his post. They were to attack at dawn, their objective the village of Seseña before moving against Torrejon. In the early morning hours of October 29th (my second birthday), Polikarpov I-15 planes strafed the enemy positions. Fifteen fast and heavily armed Russian T-26 tanks led the infantry.

From the command post, Ramón watched their troops advance under a covering artillery barrage. He hoped this would be the beginning of an offensive that would change the tide of the war. When the sector chief telephoned to report unidentified troops attacking neighboring Torrejon, Ramón's optimism faltered. Enemy bombers added more chaos to the hordes of panic-stricken militia retreating from the front. Gradually he realized that his men had attacked the wrong town and been hit by their own artillery. On the Seseña side, they had been ordered to return and defend Valdemoros from attacking troops. One by one all their morning hopes crumbled.

Lister was furious. He personally collected the scattered militia and placed them in position. The attack on Seseña, a tactical disaster, was turned into a victory by the Republican press. But the truth was that three days later Valdemoros was surrounded by the enemy and Lister's batallion had to fight their way out with bayonets and grenades.

From this point on, my father's and Lister's versions differ. Lister was outraged. They had lost ten miles. In his book *Nuestra Guerra*, he writes that, when the fight at Valdemoros seemed hopeless, Ramón left for Madrid. He goes on to complain of my father's lack of enthusiasm, of humanity, of comradeship, before accusing him of cowardice under fire and desertion from the front.

> Sender, calculating that I would not escape from the circle in which the enemy was enclosing us, retired tranquilly to his house in Madrid and, after a night's rest, presented himself at Fifth Regiment headquarters. There he displayed the commander's insignias which he said I had given him before dying. (Since I was still very much alive,) he was demoted on the spot, which was the least he merited, and his military career cut short.
>
> It then appeared that the air of Madrid no longer agreed with him and he took another 'retirement' to Barcelona and, a few weeks after, another to Paris where he 'resisted' for the rest of the war, writing his book *Counterattack* where he tells of the Seseña operation and his own personal performance, placing himself in the most advantageous position.

My father did disappear precipitously from combat during early November. The incident at headquarters may have been his desperate attempt to wrest control of the regiment from the communists and Russians who were arriving in ever greater numbers. Lister's accusations of cowardice and desertion were the most powerful insults one Spaniard could level at another. My father never responded.

Among the replies to my *El País* letter asking for information I received one from a man who had served under my father in the Shock Batallion "Commune of Madrid." He wrote he had met Sender on November 7, 1936 at the defense lines at the Manzanares River. This casts doubt on Lister's words that "his military career was cut short."

> Your father arrived at 9 P.M. in his blazing new uniform of Major (*Comandante*), and to his adjudant and po-

litical commissar he confessed his belief that Madrid
would fall in 48 hours, that there was nothing that could
be done about Franco's army. Also he had just received
news that his wife and children had been killed by the
fascists in the rebel zone. They had cut his wife's hair to
the skin, had administered castor oil and shot her as the
wife of Sender . . .

Your father wished to tell you nothing because—and
it is sad to have to tell you this—during those moments at
the front he acted as a coward; he suffered from a dreadful
fear of dying and, overpowered by terror, he disappeared
that night and left us without a commanding officer . . .

Maruchi Rivera pinpointed November 6th or 7th as the day her
father told Ramón of Amparo's death. She added that, upon hearing
this, he left immediately for France. This might well have been the
reason for his disappearance, although it seemed odd that he had not
applied for leave in the normal manner. He must have been in a
terrible state of nerves even before the news of Amparo's death
reached him, what with the Seseña fiasco and his abortive effort to
wrest control of the brigade from the communists. Could I fault
him for bizarre behavior at this point? In one letter to Joaquín
Maurín, he stated that "the Russophiles . . . now follow . . . a sys-
tematic persecution by slander." I believe the truth lay somewhere
between his and Lister's versions. The communists had been syste-
matically eliminating by whatever methods they could republican
officers who favored competing ideologies. Obviously when my father made his ill-advised attempt to take over the brigade from Lister, he was demoted and placed with another unit. At the same moment, he heard of Amparo's death and his first priority became to go
to France and recover his children. He always claimed his departure
at that moment saved his life. By his departure he avoided having
been found mysteriously shot at the Manzanares River front lines in
the days that followed.

Amparo's last message to Ramón via Pilar never reached him in
its original form. Pilar guarded it carefully until one morning the
women were lined up to be searched. Faced with forfeiting her own
life if it was discovered, she went to the bathroom, tore it into shreds
and ate it. However my father in an interview once mentioned that
he did receive a few lines Amparo had hidden among Andreina's
clothes.

In his book, *Counterattack In Spain*, my father describes how he heard that a militiaman (Victor Rivera) had arrived in Madrid and was looking for him. With an inexplicable feeling of foreboding he kept the appointment. They met at dusk at the top of the Castellana. In the distance, the clamor of machine guns increased and diminished on the freezing gusts of wind.

Victor greeted his friend with a warm embrace. "Ramón, I bring you bad news," he said. "Amparo is dead. We went to Bayonne to reclaim our children through the Red Cross, and contacted your brother's widow Marcelle as you suggested. She referred us to Dr. Marcel Junod of the International Red Cross, and through his good offices we tracked down Maruchi and Pepi in Zamora where Amparo had taken them. He managed to rescue them along with our maid Celes and we returned to Madrid with them only yesterday. They brought the terrible news of Amparo's arrest and death." He put one hand on Ramón's arm. "She died bravely, Ramón, with your name on her lips. She was denounced by her sister Casimira's husband and shot by Segundo Viloria, a member of the falange execution squad. Andreina was taken to the convent orphanage and about Monchín the only news we have is that he's safe. I know how this must pierce your heart. Believe me, it pains me to be the bearer of such news.

"Dr. Junod was unable to retrieve your children with ours because the Zamora authorities require your signed authorization. You will have to go to Bayonne and apply to the Red Cross in person."

Ramón stared across the city to the firefly flicker of the guns. "You have done me a service," he murmured at last. "At least I know the names of whom I must kill."

He walked away with rapid steps, needing time alone to allow the ice in his chest to unthaw. Why had Amparo not found safety among her family and friends? The answer condemned him with its obviousness. "I have killed her," he moaned. Grief-stricken, he stumbled bleakly onwards. His first impulse upon hearing the news had been to draw his revolver and shoot himself. But no, he would return instead to the front and take as many of the enemy as possible with him into death. Better yet, he would track the killers down one by one.

But his life was no longer his own. Amparo's death compelled him to live for the children's sake. Above and beyond any thought of revenge, he must get Andreina and Monchín to safety. He returned to the dugout that served as his command post beside the Manzanares River and lay down on his cot.

Years later he would confess his turmoil in *The Five Books Of Ariadne*, placing his words in the mouth of Javier:

"You know, Ariadne, if I express my feelings in words they vanish. For this reason I rarely spoke to you of love . . . You used to wonder, 'What does Javier think of me? Does he love me or not?' I had no idea if I did or didn't, nor did I wish to have one, because if I had told you what you meant to me, my definition would have killed those feelings . . . I didn't want to say if I loved or hated you, nor those other things which at times I was so close to saying and then said nothing . . .

"What I wanted to say to you was that in a certain way your life was of no importance to me. Don't be scandalized, my dear. I'm telling you in all seriousness, there was nothing sweeter than your thighs. Your whole body was mine. You were all mine and, in a certain way, you were my creation . . . (I see now) how your death was a distinct possibility, staying on as you did . . . but your death and your destruction seemed two separate things. I don't know if you can understand this. Perhaps there are things a woman cannot comprehend, things only a man can feel . . . Your death was not necessarily going to be your annihilation."

He could hear Amparo reply, as she always did, "This is absurd, Ramón!"

The next day, he left for Bayonne to contact Dr. Junod at the International Red Cross. At the Hotel de L'Europe he met twenty-year-old Elizabeth who would become his second wife. Their friendship blossomed around the radio in the drawing room where Ramón listened to the daily news.

Elizabeth: "I grew up with my uncle's family in Guernica. He was a Basque scholar and served several terms as mayor. When hostilities broke out in our province in the fall of 1936, we sought refuge in France."

Much to her family's disapproval, she fell in love with the radical journalist from Madrid. Ramón himself must have been swept off his feet by the remarkable beauty of this convent-educated young woman. He accompanied her on her way to Mass and back, waiting outside for the services to finish. Also he must have been motivated by his desperation to find a mother for his children.

Dr. Junod, meanwhile, returned from Zamora with us. He brought me immediately to Bayonne while Andrea remained in San Juan de Luz because of a severe skin rash that had to be treated before she could enter France. My old aunt Maximina met with my father and delivered to him a letter from Amparo which had been found among Andrea's clothes by the nuns in the orphanage.

It was a hurried farewell in which she recommended he marry a friend of hers in Madrid who she felt would care for us as her own.

"Ah, no! She's much too ugly!" he replied, according to Maximina's report to the family in Zamora.

Elizabeth: "You were very traumatized when Dr. Junod brought you to us. Very withdrawn. Your father and I took you almost at once to your Aunt Maruja's in Barcelona. On the flight from Toulouse you kept saying, 'I want to get off,' much to your father's amusement. He returned immediately to wait for your sister."

Marcelle: "What you, Ramón, liked best was to ride the trams in Bayonne. Your sister came later. The wetnurse who had come with her was not given permission to exit Spain. Because of this, a cousin of mine who had recently had a baby breast-fed her. Also we began bottle-feeding her. Poor little thing, she never cried and was so very small. My father loved children and played a great deal with her. She used to laugh when he caught her by the fingers. And my father would say, 'How can she know, poor sweetheart, what has happened?'

Elizabeth: "After your father arrived in Barcelona with Andrea, we were married at the end of December before a member of the Catalan parliament. Our witnesses were your Aunt Maruja and my brother Sabino. My family only agreed to the civil ceremony because there were no priests in Barcelona at the time, and because Ramón promised a church ceremony when we left Spain. We departed immediately with you children for Pau, France, where Ramón rented a furnished apartment on Blackbeard Boulevard. He had signed a contract with an English editor to write the book *The War In Spain* (entitled *Counterattack In Spain* in the American edition). He dictated it to me and I took it down in shorthand."

At the beginning of 1937 we moved to a cottage in Louvie-Juzon, a picturesque village close to the frontier of Aragon. My father wrote another book there, probably *A Man's Place*. In November, Elizabeth gave birth to Emmanuel. During that winter my father made two trips to Paris to help with the International Congress of Writers.

Also he travelled to the United States in April 1938, on a fund-raising tour for the Republic.

Elizabeth: "Andrea was very sweet, very adorable. She was much more trusting than Monchín. Monchín was very different, because he had participated in the drama. In June, Ramón returned from Barcelona and told me the war was lost. He would return to the front 'to strike a last blow,' but we could not go on living together. In the same manner as Amparo, he told me to go to my father's house in Barcelona. I left at the beginning of June 1938, and since that time I lost all trace of him and you children."

"In the same manner as Amparo . . ." The coincidence was indeed strange. And why did he send Elizabeth and his infant son back to Spain when, in his own words, "the war was lost?"

Papá took Andrea and me to Paris briefly before placing us in "Duremont," a camp in Calais for Spanish refugee children. Andrea almost died of pneumonia that winter. Meanwhile, he struck up a relationship with a Viennese journalist named Anya Herzog whom Elizabeth felt might have been the true reason for his abandonment of her. Now that my memory had been jogged, I recalled an attractive blonde coming with Papá to the camp for visits.

In March of 1939, Papá booked passage on the USS *Manhattan* and brought us to New York. He left us with Jay Allen and his wife Ruth. He had met Allen during his stint as correspondent in Spain for the *Chicago Tribune*. He also left a note which described me as obedient and gentle if my wishes were respected. If I became obstinate, it was best to leave me alone. My experiences had given me a timidity which did not represent my real character, yet my sense of beauty, of color, of nature and music, were enormously developed. Andrea he described as the opposite of me, very sociable and open; but he warned against spoiling her because then she became a tyrant. She should be spoken to gently but with authority. "When you talk to them about me," he finished, "I beg you to tell them that I have gone to Mexico to buy them a little house."

Ramón J. Sender. Circa 1950.

Ramón and Andrea (Benedicta) in Washington Square Park during their stay with the Jay Allens in March 1939. Ramón is four and a half, and Benedicta is three.

Ramón at six and Andrea (Benedicta) at four, at Julia Davis's home in Bedford Village, 1941.

Left to right: *Ramón, Andrea (Benedicta), Julia Davis, Florence Hall Sender (Ramón J. Sender's third wife), Charles P. Healy (Julia's third husband), and Ramón J. Sender. Summer 1951. Photograph by Erin Healy.*

EPILOGUE

Upon our return to the States from Spain in August 1982, my wife and I stopped on the East Coast to visit my American mother Julia in the Berkshires. She and her husband were delighted to see us, tired after a busy summer of grandchildren and putting up vegetables from the garden. At 82 and 86 years respectively, it was no longer easy to do everything they would like.

"I have to remind myself I'm no longer a young girl of seventy," Julia told me with a twinkle in her eye.

She was relieved that my trip to Spain was not as emotionally stressful as my sister's. I explained it had been just the opposite. True, the journey had been painful at times, but in a good way like the excising of a boil. For so many years I had lived not knowing, not experiencing the part of me that had suffered through the death of my mother. The presence of my wife and her language skills helped me enormously. Without her, the terrors of the past might have overwhelmed me. Instead, she was always beside me with her love and understanding. In a way the trip was harder for her because she was not experiencing the healing of a wound but just hearing the grim details over and over.

Standing left to right: *Casimira Barayón (Amparo's oldest half-sister), Miguel Sevilla (Casimira's husband who denounced Amparo to the fascists), sister Nati Barayón.* Seated: *Amparo, approximately twelve years old here. Estimated date of photograph is 1916.*

Also, I returned with a deepened appreciation of Julia's mothering, of how much she gave me. Before our departure, I wrote her a note: 'No matter how much I have rediscovered Amparo, I am also your son.'

So much of a child's remembrance depended on continuity, on the adults saying, 'Remember when . . .' or paging through the family photo album together. On the first page of ours, beneath Amparo's passport portrait, was one of two children in white sunsuits glowering at the camera. For years I had assumed it was taken in Barcelona, but looking at it now I recognized the cottage in Louvie-Juzon. Benedicta recently removed the one of Amparo and found a dedication scrawled across the back:

> 'To my Ramón, with the madness of madnesses, with
> all my enthusiasm and more. Always more!!
> Your Frisky Little Goat'

Another photo Benedicta unearthed for me showed Amparo as a young girl seated in front of Miguel Sevilla, Casimira and Nati. The three older people are dressed in black, perhaps in mourning for their father in 1918. Amparo looks as if she could well be thirteen, just passing into adolescence. Sevilla and Casimira are staring into each others' eyes, Sevilla with a cigar in one hand, the camera case dangling from the other. Casimira wears a black veil over her hat, and glances up at Sevilla adoringly. Meanwhile his pose expresses a condescending acceptance of her homage, as if he was thinking, 'You aren't really what I had in mind for someone as deserving as myself, but at least there's the café and the ice house.' His back is turned to Nati who stands frozen to the spot by some inner agony. Her eyelids droop, her hands are clenched, her mouth expressionless. Obviously she is not a well person.

In the foreground, light bathes Amparo in contrast to the darkness that afflicts the others. She is dressed in white and holds what looks like a prayerbook. Rows of lace on the sleeves and a colored sash adorn her dress. Her Sunday best—they must have been on their way home from church. Her hair is done up in pigtails, one strand dangling over her forehead. The corners of her full lips form the first creases of a smile, mischief lurking just under the surface. 'I'm not going to laugh,' she is thinking.

Casimira and Sevilla pose as if they are the only ones having their picture taken. Sevilla has the self-satisfied expression of a man fixated on himself. The upper part of his profile is cleancut, but a self-indulgent puffiness distorts the area above the mouth and the lower lip curls disdainfully. Nati might not exist as far as he is concerned, although her right arm almost touches him.

Here were the people who destroyed Amparo and her family: Casimira with her blind adulation of Sevilla, Sevilla who would stop at nothing to take control of the inheritance, and poor, deaf Nati whose frail mind would crumble after the murders. Her medical needs compelled everyone except Casimira to renounce the family property.

In the midst of these shadowy forces poised over her, Amparo sat as fresh-faced and fragrant as a carnation. Her strength was in her softness, her vulnerability, her ability to love. Even if this book had never been written, Amparo's story would have outlived the sordidness of her betrayers' lives. Our immortality may exist only within the memories of the loved ones we leave behind.

Miguel and Casimira Sevilla moved away from Zamora and settled in Seville to distance themselves from their guilt. What about the other villains? Viloria died insane in a state institution. The military governor lived out his years in Zamora with only a grandson to question his actions. Perhaps an aged Catholic priest in a village named Paradinas occasionally frets about the disposition of his soul.

In one of the rare references my father ever made to Amparo, he wrote:

> I have discovered what the moralists call 'the feminine soul' (how I despise that term!) only in one woman: Amparo. She whom I loved was a physical being and yet, nevertheless, immortal. Physically immortal.

For once, my father and I can agree. Amparo had finally brought us, father and son, full circle.

BIBLIOGRAPHY

JULIA DAVIS. *The Sun Climbs Slow*, E.P. Dutton & Co. Inc., New York, 1942. A fictional treatment of our arrival in Julia's life, although many of the scenes with the children are accurate portrayals.

PILAR FIDALGO. *A Young Mother in Franco's Prisons*, United Editorial Ltd., London, 1939. A major source of information on the conditions in the women's cell in Zamora. The Southworth Collection at the University of California, San Diego has a copy.

PILAR FIDALGO. *Nine Months in the Hands of the Fascists, A Personal Testimony, El Socialista*, May 20, 21, 22, 1937, Madrid. Testimony Pilar Fidalgo gave before the Spanish consul in Bayonne shortly after she was repatriated from Zamora.

ENRIQUE LISTER. *Nuestra Guerra*, Colección Ebro, Editions de la Librairie du Globe, Paris, 1966. Lister's colorful autobiography as the communist ironworker who evolved into one of the Republic's top military leaders during the Civil War. I quote his opinion of Ramón J. Sender.

JOAQUÍN MAURÍN Letter to Ramón J. Sender, from the large collection of Maurín/Sender correspondence in the Archives of The Hoover Institute, Palo Alto.

RAMÓN J. SENDER. Letters to Joaquín Maurín, Archives of The Hoover Institute, Palo Alto.

RAMÓN J. SENDER. *Los Cinco Libros De Ariadna*, Ediciones Destino, Barcelona, 1977. My father always referred to this novel when I asked him for details of Amparo's childhood. I have translated selections that seemed appropriate. Also it contained important information on their last hours together in San Rafael.

RAMÓN J. SENDER. *Selecciones De Poesia Lirica Y Aforistica*, bilingual edition with translations by Florence Talamantes, El Sol de California, San Diego, 1979. His sonnet to Amparo is included.

RAMÓN J. SENDER. *Seven Red Sundays*, Liveright Publishing Co., New York, 1936. An early novel set during a proletarian uprising in Madrid. It recounts the tale of Amparo's placing of a bomb in the telephone building.

RAMÓN J. SENDER. *The War in Spain*, Faber & Faber Ltd. London, 1937 *Counterattack in Spain* in the American edition, Houghton Mifflin Company, Boston, 1937. An autobiographical account of the author's activities during the first six months of the civil war. I have utilized it as a source for the chapter on my father.

SUGGESTED READING

HUGH THOMAS. *The Spanish Civil War*, Harper & Row, Revised & Enlarged Edition, New York, 1977.

GABRIEL JACKSON. *The Spanish Republic & The Civil War*, Princeton University Press, 1965.

RONALD FRASER. *The Blood of Spain, An Oral History of the Spanish Civil War*, Pantheon Books, New York, 1979.

DAN KURZMAN. *Miracle of November, Madrid's Epic Stand*, G.T. Putnam's Sons, New York, 1980.

GEORGE HILLS. *The Battle for Madrid*, St. Martin's Press, New York, 1977

CLAUDE G. BOWERS. *My Mission to Spain*, Simon & Schuster, New York, 1954.

ARTURO BAREA. *The Forging of a Rebel*, David-Poynter Ltd., London, 1972.

FREDERICK BENSON. *Writers in Arms*, New York University Press, New York, 1967.

ROBERT A. ROSENSTONE. *Crusade on the Left*, Pegasus, New York, 1969.

Grateful acknowledgment is made for permission to quote from the following:

Los Cinco Libros de Ariadna by Ramón J. Sender, copyright 1977 by Ediciones Destino, Barcelona. Excerpts translated by Ramón Sender Barayón with permission of the publisher.

Letters from Ramón J. Sender to Joaquin Maurín. Excerpts translated by Ramón Sender Barayón with permission of Mrs. Jeanne Maurín. Also a letter from Joaquin Maurín to Ramón J. Sender.

A Young Mother in Franco's Prisons by Pilar Fidalgo. Quoted by permission of the author.

Library of Congress Cataloging-in-Publication Data

Sender Barayón, Ramón, 1934–
    A death in Zamora / Ramón Sender Barayón
        p.   cm.
    Bibliography: p.
    ISBN 0-8263-1139-3
    1. Sender, Ramón José, 1901–1982. 2. Novelists, Spanish—20th century—Biography. 3. Barayón, Amparo, 1904–1936. 4. Wives—Spain—Biography. 5. Barayón family. 6. Spain—History—Civil War, 1936–1939. 7. Sender Barayón, Ramón, 1934–   . I. Title.
PQ6635.E65Z83   1989
863'.62—dc19
[B]   88-36824

Design by Susan Gutnik